D1313491

Investigating
SHERLOCK

The Unofficial Guide
NIKKI STAFFORD

MYRMIDON

Published by Myrmidon
Rotterdam House
116 Quayside
Newcastle upon Tyne
England
NE1 3DY

A CATALOGUE RECORD FOR THIS BOOK
IS AVAILABLE FROM THE BRITISH LIBRARY.
ISBN 978-1-910183-18-2

Available as an ebook
[ISBN 978-1-910183-19-9]

Editor: Crissy Calhoun
Cover design: Michel Vrana
Cover image: Aleksandra Lech
(www.behance.net/aleksandralech)
London Skyline: Freepik.com
Interior illustrations: Troy Cunningham

Printed in the UK by CPI Group (UK) Ltd,
Croydon, CR0 4YY

1 3 5 7 9 8 6 4 2

For Sydney and Liam,
my own little Holmes and Watson
(though I've yet to determine which is which)

SPOILER WARNING

While I won't outright spoil future episodes, I have written this book with the assumption that most readers have watched all of *Sherlock*, and I will therefore hint at some things to come. I recommend that you watch the entire season before reading the corresponding guide to that season.

"EVERYTHING HAD CHANGED IN 90 MINUTES"
The Genesis of *Sherlock*

According to Arthur Conan Doyle biographer Russell Miller, only Mickey Mouse and Santa Claus rival Sherlock Holmes for worldwide instant recognition. The great detective holds the world record for most movie adaptations of a single fictional character. Almost 130 years after he was first invented, he remains the most popular fictional detective of all time. He is instantly recognizable when seen in silhouette form. And yet, since William Gillette first walked onto a London stage in 1899 as Sherlock Holmes, everyone who has ever stepped into Holmes's shoes has brought something new to the character. Basil Rathbone emphasized the character's quiet dignity, Jeremy Brett his cunning intensity and humor. Robert Downey Jr.'s Holmes is a bare-knuckle boxer and man of action (which, as might come as a surprise to some, is actually one aspect of the Holmes character in the books). There have been parodies and pastiches, fan fiction and fan speculation. Was there really room for yet another version of the great detective?

What a ridiculous question.

Two of the greatest moments of inspiration in British pop culture have happened on trains: on a long trip from Manchester to London, J.K. Rowling scribbled on a napkin the beginnings of the idea for a series of books about a boy wizard. And throughout several shorter trips from Cardiff to London, *Doctor Who* writers Steven Moffat and Mark Gatiss talked about their love of the Sherlock Holmes stories and wondered why no one had developed a modern-day version for television.

In both cases, the rest is history.

Steven Moffat (born November 18, 1961) is the son of schoolteachers, and he followed them into the same profession while writing on the side. Moffat's father, Bill, pitched a series to a BBC executive about a school newspaper, and they loved it. Bill said they could have it — on the grounds that they take a look at his schoolteacher son's pilot script. They loved it, and the sitcom *Press Gang* (1989–1993) was born. Moffat wrote all 43 episodes of the show, which took a toll on both him and his marriage. Two more sitcoms followed — *Joking Apart* and *Chalk* — followed by his breakout hit, *Coupling*, where he again wrote every episode. Where *Press Gang* and *Joking Apart* featured scenes from his own dissolving marriage, *Coupling* (2000–2004)

2

took conversations and situations directly from his burgeoning relationship with Sue Vertue, a producer at the BBC. The two eventually married and have two sons.

In 1999, Moffat wrote *The Curse of Fatal Death*, a parody of his favorite show, *Doctor Who*. The fake episode, done for Comic Relief, starred Rowan Atkinson (among others) as the Doctor. When the series was rebooted by the BBC in 2005, with Russell T Davies at the helm as the showrunner, Steven Moffat quickly became a beloved writer among fans. Penning such episodes as "The Empty Child/The Doctor Dances," "The Girl in the Fireplace," "Blink," and "Silence in the Library/Forest of the Dead," he became known as the darker writer, creating the terrifying Weeping Angels and making the phrase "Are you my mummy?" send chills down the spines of every Whovian. He is credited with bringing some of the spookier aspects of *Doctor Who* back to the fore, which, he says, were his favorite bits when he was a child watching it from behind his sofa. *"Doctor Who,"* he says, "is how we warn our children that there are people in the world who want to eat them."

Because of the show filming in both Cardiff and London, Moffat had to constantly travel between the two places, and often did so with his fellow writer and friend Mark Gatiss.

Gatiss (born October 17, 1966) had a unique upbringing. When the Durham mines closed, his miner father went to work with Gatiss's mother at a psychiatric hospital, the Aycliffe Colony for the Mentally Defective. Gatiss spent a lot of his free time at the hospital, using the facilities and even watching films at the hospital's cinema. He recalls that sitting amongst people whose illnesses "left deep marks on their faces" was so frightening, he could barely focus on the movies. He attributes his later interest in monsters and demons to these early experiences.

Gatiss went off to drama college and met Reece Shearsmith, Jeremy Dyson, and Steve Pemberton, with whom he formed the League of Gentlemen dark comedy troupe, which inspired a wacky BBC2 television series in the late 1990s about a group of strange people who live in the Yorkshire Moors. To supplement his income, he wrote *Doctor Who* novels (having been a fan of the show since he was a boy), and he came on board the TV series in 2005, penning such episodes as "The Unquiet Dead," "The Idiot's Lantern," "Night Terrors," and "The Crimson Horror." In 2008, he married his longtime partner, Ian Hallard.

Around the same time, during one of those train rides to Cardiff, the topic moved from Time Lords to Great Detectives. "We'd been friends for years anyway," says Moffat, "but we'd often been getting the train together . . . and the main thing we kept saying, was that someone should do what they did with Rathbone again. Someone should do it modern day — do the stories, not the trappings. And I said that to Sue [Vertue, producer], I said, 'Someone should do that, and it's really annoying because it should be us,' and she said, 'Why don't you?'" Gatiss and Moffat began discussing the idea more seriously, and soon realized that a modernized version could actually work, simply because of the similarities between the present day and the Victorian era.

"One of the wonderful, easy ways into this as an idea, and to explain to other people, is that in the very first, original story, Dr. Watson is invalided home from Afghanistan," says Gatiss. "And it's the same unwinnable war, virtually. Once you start thinking like that, the whole show makes total sense." Sir Arthur Conan Doyle wrote his Sherlock Holmes stories in an era that was exploding with innovation and a culture that was undergoing drastic changes. Science was causing people to question their religious beliefs, technology was starting to change the way everyday tasks were done, and the economy was on an upswing as England found balance decades after the Industrial Revolution. Fast-forward to the 2000s, where the century was jumpstarted by the confusing and world-altering events of September 11th, where scientific achievements continue to move at the speed of light, and where technology is exploding at such a rate that one can date what year a television episode or movie is set purely based on the characters' cellphones.

Gatiss and Moffat were not the only ones who could see the connection between Victorian Holmes and the modern day. From 2004 to 2012, *House, M.D.* was one of the top-rated shows on television, featuring a doctor with a drug problem solving rare medical cases while maintaining a cold exterior — in other words, Holmes in a hospital. In 2009, Guy Ritchie released his first of two gritty, bombastic, action-packed versions of the Sherlock Holmes stories, starring Robert Downey Jr. as the detective and Jude Law as the doctor. It was set in the Victorian era, but had a distinctly 21st-century vibe. Soon after *Sherlock* began, NBC greenlit another modern-day Sherlock Holmes in *Elementary*, with British actor Jonny Lee Miller in the role of the great detective, transposed to New York City as a recovering addict living with his "sober companion," Dr. Joan Watson (Lucy Liu).

Where the other modernized versions of Sherlock Holmes used the idea of the character but not the actual stories, Gatiss and Moffatt were suggesting something new: a show that would take the traditional Sherlock Holmes stories and translate them to a 21st-century sensibility, which, given the similarities between the two eras, wouldn't be a stretch at all. "I would say to anyone who is worried that it has to be about hansom cabs and fogs," says Gatiss, "it so doesn't. It's about the relationship between these two unlikely friends, and the adventures they have. And it works."

The contracts were put together and the BBC greenlit the first season as three 90-minute episodes (as opposed to six 60-minute episodes, as Moffat and Gatiss had proposed). The showrunners wanted their Holmes to be different from those of Basil Rathbone and Jeremy Brett; for inspiration, they both turned to their preferred Sherlock Holmes adaptation: the 1970 Billy Wilder film, *The Private Life of Sherlock Holmes*. They took two key things from that film, the first being its humor. "Very often Sherlock Holmes is not funny," says Moffat. "The books are funny! The interaction between the two characters is always funny. It's a weird genius and an ordinary not-genius." In one Doyle story, for example, Watson begins with a threat to one particular reader who he believes has been attempting to break into their home to destroy files: "The source of these outrages is known," he writes angrily, "and if they are repeated I have Mr. Holmes's authority for saying that the whole story concerning the politician, the lighthouse, and the trained cormorant will be given to the public. There is at least one reader who will understand."

The second aspect of *The Private Life of Sherlock Holmes* that the co-creators wanted to incorporate into their show was the friendship between Holmes and Watson. Where other adaptations often presented Holmes as the genius and Watson as the silly bumbler, Wilder showed them in a friendship of equals, which was what Gatiss and Moffat believed Sir Arthur Conan Doyle had intended when he wrote the stories. "When Steven Moffat and I came up with the idea of a modern-day Sherlock Holmes," says Gatiss, "it was crucial to us that the series be regarded as a co-lead. It's called *Sherlock*, but the great detective's enduring friendship with his Boswell is the beating heart that has kept the stories so popular for more than 120 years." They also wanted there to be a deeper level of intimacy between the two men, something they thought was Doyle's intention, even if his language had to remain coy because of the era in which he wrote. Gatiss likes to reference a moment in Arthur Conan Doyle's Holmes story "The Yellow Face" as being a key influence in the way they write the two friends: "Nothing's happening in the case, and Holmes is moping. Watson eventually persuades him to come out of the house for a walk. And he writes, 'We rambled about together, in silence for the most part, as befits two men who know each other intimately.' I've never forgotten that."

Only one person was auditioned for the part of Sherlock, and that was Benedict Cumberbatch. Steven Moffat and Sue Vertue invited Cumberbatch to the apartment of Sue's mother, Beryl Vertue, a legendary television producer and agent. As he was beginning his audition, Beryl came in bearing a tray with tea and biscuits. Cumberbatch pointed to her and said, "Is she playing Mrs. Hudson?" "No," replied Sue. "That's my mother." He got the part anyway.

The part of John Watson, on the other hand, was more difficult to cast. Martin Freeman has explained in many an interview that he was having a particularly bad morning the day of his audition, and when he showed up to read for the part, Moffat assumed he wasn't actually interested in it. When that was conveyed to Freeman's agent, Freeman asked for another chance and came in to read opposite Cumberbatch.

"I had a superb audition with Martin," says Benedict, "and I immediately knew that he was my primary choice. He was definitely the person that I immediately sparked off and raised my game for. He's an adorable man and blissfully, ridiculously funny and entertaining. He's a great support and companion in real life as well. We have tremendous fun doing the show."

They knew then that they'd found their Watson. Interestingly, a young man named Matt Smith also came in to read for the part of the doctor, but was turned down as not being quite right for it. A week later he auditioned for the part of a Time Lord, and became a Doctor after all.

Because so much of *Doctor Who* is filmed in Cardiff, it made sense to do *Sherlock* there as well. While the exterior doorway and street of 221B Baker Street is actually in London (incidentally, on North Gower Street, not on Baker), the interior stairwell and set of the flat itself is in Cardiff. Next time you're watching an episode, pay attention to the way the shot transitions from the stairwell to the street outside: the two spots are 150 miles apart, despite appearing to be adjoined.

Everyone had fun filming the first series; at the time, Benedict Cumberbatch had done some major roles in the theater and had starred in *Hawking*, but was otherwise relatively unknown, playing character roles in various film and television series. Martin Freeman, on the other hand, was recognizable for his internationally acclaimed role as Tim Canterbury on *The Office*. Both men first settled in to read the books to fully become these two iconic characters of English literature. For Cumberbatch, turning to the source material was essential. Like Gatiss and Moffat, Cumberbatch had been reading the Sherlock Holmes stories since he was a boy. "I would have been about 12 years old when I first read it, and I was hungry for more," he remembers. "It's just very addictive reading, and it's an utterly absorbing world. It's thrilling, as a child, to read those books. You get drawn into a London which suddenly becomes alive like a pop-up book, but brilliant in this other era. It's just a really rich tapestry of characters and extraordinary adventures."

The onscreen chemistry between Cumberbatch and Freeman was perfection. Freeman in particular appreciated how Gatiss and Moffat had interpreted his character from the books. "What I love about our John Watson is that even though there is humor in him, it's a straight part, and it's a straight program. No one is a buffoon in it, and what I really like about it is that it's writing for grown-ups, where you're not having to cheat the audience. I'm purely trying to play this part the way I approach everything, which is to be truthful. I was trying to make Watson a feasible soldier, a feasible doctor. I wanted to give him a strength and a vulnerability."

Cumberbatch liked the challenge of playing a character that was a hero, yet so unlikable. He doesn't kid himself that Sherlock has a dark side. "I always make it clear that people who become obsessed with him or the idea of him — he'd destroy you . . . He is an absolute bastard." Watson, on the other hand, balances the relationship through his dependability. "I think the defining thing about Dr. Watson in all his incarnations is that he's the first man a genius would trust," Moffat says. "Sherlock sees a reliability and a complete trustworthiness in this honest, good man."

The rest of the cast is equally stunning: Una Stubbs as Mrs. Hudson is wonderful, a landlady and housekeeper who insists she is *not* a housekeeper, who mothers the boys in such a way that they come to love her and be annoyed by her in equal parts, as one often does with one's mother. In the books Inspector Lestrade is usually referred to as being a slimy, small, weasel-like creature who uses Holmes and then takes credit for the cases, but on the show Rupert Graves plays Lestrade as a gruff man who calls in Sherlock on the difficult cases because he respects him, even if begrudgingly. Molly Hooper is a complete fabrication with no equivalent in the books, which was something Gatiss and Moffat had sworn they wouldn't do: there would be no recurring characters who weren't already part of the Doyle canon. The problem was, actress Louise Brealey had done such a spectacular job as the morgue registrar who has an unrequited crush on the great detective that the creators couldn't help themselves; they had to bring her back again and again. Aside from Mrs. Hudson, we don't see Holmes having much to do with women outside of the cases, and introducing Molly allows us to see his half-assed attempts to actually deal with a woman.

But despite all of the parts coming together so beautifully, no one could have predicted just how massive the show was going to be upon its premiere.

On the evening of July 25, 2010, Moffat, Gatiss, Sue Vertue, Cumberbatch, and Freeman all gathered at Moffat's house to watch the premiere of *Sherlock*. Cumberbatch showed up late, calling to say he was stuck in a traffic jam on Baker Street — "I think he might have made that up, to be honest," Gatiss says, "but it's a really good lie" — and so they began watching it ten minutes behind the rest of the country. However, they knew the moment when everyone else had finished the episode, because their phones started ringing ten minutes before they were done.

"An hour later, I went and sat in the garden," Moffat says, "and looked at Twitter. I saw that Benedict was trending world-wide on Twitter, Martin was trending worldwide, *Sherlock* itself was trending worldwide. And people were talking about it with this . . . passion. As if they were lifelong fans — when, of course, they'd not seen it 90 minutes ago. Everything had changed in 90 minutes."

When the show premiered in North America in October, it was an instant success. By the time filming for season two began, the atmosphere was very different on set. This time they knew they had a bona fide hit, and by tackling Sherlock's three biggest foes in a single season — the Woman, the Hound, and the Professor — they knew fans would be whipped into a frenzy.

Meanwhile, by the second season Cumberbatch's star was on the rise, having appeared in Steven Spielberg's *War Horse* and the British spy drama *Tinker Tailor Soldier Spy*, while Freeman's turn as Bilbo Baggins in *The Hobbit: An Unexpected Journey* was about to send him into the celebrity stratosphere. For Cumberbatch, returning to the set for season two was a different experience than when they were beginning season one. "It felt awkward, actually, coming back the first time. Not because it was strange but in a way because it had been such a success. I think we both felt slightly that we were outside of it, looking in. I was looking at Martin Freeman and thinking: 'God, I saw you on the telly in something rather good during the summer.' It took a little bit of time to get the rhythm and pacing back, partly because of what had happened in the meantime."

Plus, of course, there was that whole thing with . . . *the hair*. Not just that his natural reddish-brown locks had to be dyed black, but that they had to be longer. "I was short and blond in *Tinker Tailor Soldier Spy*," says Cumberbatch, "and I really, really didn't like coming back to this hair for this second series. I can't think of a wittier or even accurate comparison, but I just think it makes me look a bit like . . . a woman."

The second season ended on a giant cliffhanger that caused fan theories to pop up everywhere: how were the writers going to work their way out of such an explosive ending? By the beginning of season three, more than 10,000 American fans entered a competition to win one of 150 tickets to a New York screening of the third season premiere. The BBC ran all three episodes of season three between January 1 and January 12, 2014. Over 12 million viewers tuned in to the episodes.

There was some concern over the addition of Mary Morstan in the show's third outing: would a new character come between the two men and ruin the dynamic the fans had come to love?

Amanda Abbington, Martin Freeman's real-life partner, was cast in the role . . . and immediately began feeling the heat. "When I told everybody that I was playing Mary, there was a small group who wanted me dead," she says. "I got, 'She should die. How dare she play Mary Morstan? How dare she!' They take the John and Sherlock storyline so seriously that they wouldn't want anyone coming between them." Cumberbatch thought she entered the dynamic seamlessly, making Sherlock act differently around her. "He still exists in his own limelight and he's not smothered by that relationship," he says. "But she's an incredibly strong female character. She's very involved and that's brilliant. I love the dynamic. Amanda is just astonishingly subtle and has sublime good taste as an actress. She's really special."

Over three seasons and four years, the writing has become tighter, the chemistry between the actors and characters stronger, and the show has reinvented how the world sees Sherlock Holmes and Dr. Watson. Martin Freeman is thrilled by it: "It's developed like any other relationship. By the end of the first series, you saw John and Sherlock's friendship move on: I went from being just purely agog at everything he did, to being quite pissed off at some of the things he did. That road is explored further in [season two]. But it's become more of a partnership. John is now only half a step behind Sherlock, as opposed to six steps."

Meanwhile, Moffat and Gatiss must now work around Freeman's and Cumberbatch's nearly impossible schedules as Cumberbatch takes on several films at once while Freeman starred in a second television series — *Fargo* — between Hobbit sequels. All the while, the two writers continue to work for that *other* BBC show. Writing for two shows at once, Gatiss and Moffat are often asked if they ever mix up the two iconic British figures of the Doctor and Sherlock Holmes. Despite the Time

Lord being an alien from Gallifrey, Moffat laughs, "I think the Doctor is more human. I think he's more playful, and more ordinary and more distractible. They are sort of opposite. The Doctor is an alien, a remote outsider, who aspires to be one of us. He likes playing around with us. And Sherlock Holmes aspires to be a Time Lord."

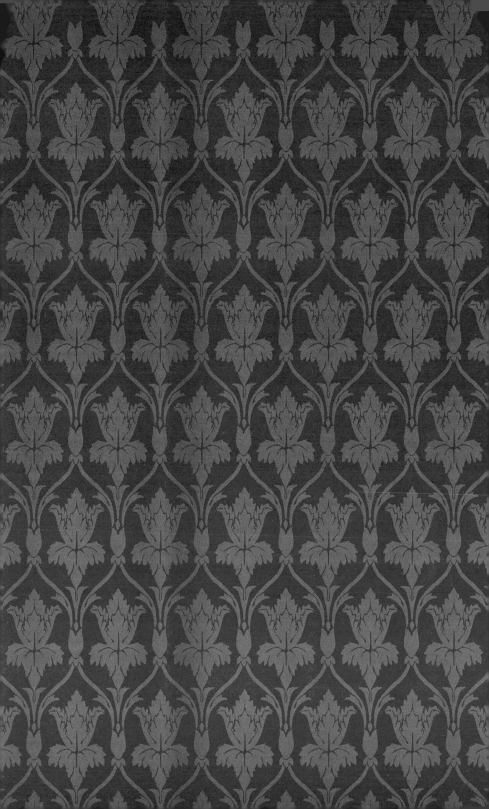

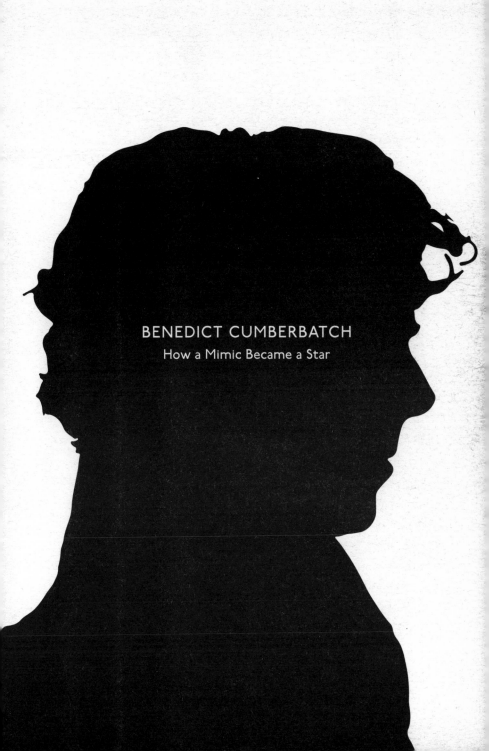

BENEDICT CUMBERBATCH

How a Mimic Became a Star

He has the best name in show business (which he describes as sounding "like a fart in a bath"), and might be the single most educated actor on television, but friends of the man the *Washington Post* once called "Bandersnatch Cummerbund" have discovered that he can be easily pranked. When Simon Pegg, his co-star on *Star Trek Into Darkness*, convinced Benedict Cumberbatch to apply a face cream to protect himself against radiation due to the fact they were filming in a nuclear facility, the actor not only complied, but later apologized to the other actors when he flubbed his lines, explaining, "I think the ions were getting to me."

Benedict Timothy Carlton Cumberbatch was born on July 19, 1976, to parents Timothy Carlton (who dropped the "Cumberbatch" for professional reasons) and Wanda Ventham. Both parents are actors — Carlton in the theater, Ventham in television shows (including three spots on *Doctor Who*) and films, as well as several theater productions.

And yes, Ventham and Carlton play Sherlock's parents on the show.

At age eight, Cumberbatch went off to boarding school before becoming an arts scholar at the prestigious Harrow School (which has been referred to as the Yale to Eton's Harvard). He bristles now at the notion that he somehow had a posh upbringing, explaining that his parents were working actors who did not come from a lot of money. He didn't go to Harrow because of a mountain of wealth, but because of his own intelligence and hard work, acing the entrance exams and attending on a scholarship. He loved being surrounded by the other boys; Cumberbatch is an only child, with a half-sister from Ventham's first marriage who is 18 years his senior.

As a child he was fascinated with other voices and trying to imitate them. For a short time he carried a Dictaphone around with him, recording people talking and then practicing their voices until he could do remarkable impersonations of them. He studied mannerisms, imitating the way people moved and carried themselves, a skill he still uses today when playing historical figures such as Alan Turing, Julian Assange, or Stephen Hawking. "I had a problem focusing," he explains now. "I probably had attention deficit disorder, or something on the border of it. I was always performing, doing silly voices. The teachers realized I could go on one of two ways: be creative or destructive. I was made a prefect and it calmed me down. I realized I was being respected and I needed to return that respect."

The Dictaphone soon disappeared, and Benedict began using his talents for good, joining the drama program. As a child he had wanted to be a barrister until he was told that most of the job was simply chasing down the next paycheck, and he decided acting would be easier, especially if he was already showing a talent for it. Because it was an all-boy's school, some of his earliest roles were as women. "I was Titania [Queen of the Fairies] in *A Midsummer Night's Dream* when I was 13," he says. "I did a good enough job to get the part of Rosalind [in *As You Like It*] the next year. I was a very late developer."

After graduating from Harrow, he spent a year teaching English at a Tibetan monastery before attending the University of Manchester to take his undergraduate degree in drama, followed by a graduate degree in classical acting at the prestigious London Academy of Music and Dramatic Art. He knew he'd made it as an actor after a university performance of *Amadeus*, when his father came backstage to congratulate him on playing the part of Salieri. Cumberbatch says, "He looked me in the eye and grabbed me by the shoulders and said, 'You're better now than I ever was or will be. I think you'll have a wonderful life and career as an actor, and I can't wait to be a part of watching it.' And I pretty much burst into tears. What a huge thing for a man to say to his son. I mean, not only an actor to an actor, but to give me that sort of 'I bless this ship and all who sail upon her' kind of a message."

From there Cumberbatch went on to do a lot of work on the London stage, appearing in such classic plays as *Love's Labour's Lost* in 2001 and *Hedda Gabler* in 2005. After some small parts in television shows, in 2004 he starred as Stephen Hawking in the BBC television production of *Hawking*, about the theoretical physicist's early years at Cambridge and the beginnings of his struggle with ALS. Cumberbatch received widespread acclaim, and he was nominated for a BAFTA TV award the following year. Over the next few years, he was the go-to "where do I know that guy from?" for North American audiences as he appeared in films such as *Starter for 10*, *Atonement*, *The Other Boleyn Girl*, and *Tinker Tailor Soldier Spy*.

It almost didn't happen, though. While filming the television miniseries *To the Ends of the Earth* in South Africa in 2005, Cumberbatch was taking a day trip with some friends when they got a flat tire and pulled to the side of the road. They suddenly found themselves surrounded by a group of men who looted the car, tied up Cumberbatch and his friends, threw him into the trunk of their car, and drove to another location, where they lined them up on the ground and held a gun to the back of Cumberbatch's head, execution style. Cumberbatch immediately began talking, and in a moment that could have been taken right out of *Sherlock*, he managed to talk the kidnappers out of killing them, and they were released. The next morning, rather than traumatized by the events of the day, he found himself happy to be alive and determined to live a more exciting life. "I want to go out and swim and run through the sand dunes and into that landscape," he recalls thinking. "It was a small event in a big country."

In 2010, he read for the part of a lifetime when he was asked to meet with Steven Moffat and Mark Gatiss. It was a daunting task, not least because actors such as Basil Rathbone, Peter Cushing, and Jeremy Brett had defined the popular perception of Holmes through their performances. Jeremy Brett, whom many consider to be the ultimate Holmes, was even more intimidating for Benedict because he'd been a family friend. "He casts a towering shadow," Cumberbatch says. "He was a friend of my mom's, and he was around our family a lot. He and the part collided, and he let it take him over." Once Martin Freeman was cast as the Watson to Cumberbatch's Holmes, the next hurdle was learning how to deliver the lines the way Gatiss and Moffat wanted, which was true to the books but so close to impossible that no other actor had done it at such a breakneck speed. "It's a huge challenge to learn and perform at [that] speed," he says. "It takes time and an awful lot of takes sometimes, but it's like music, you can hear when it's right or wrong and it's a fantastic feeling when it flies, as there is no thinking time to be self conscious about the choices you're making, it's all about driving it forward so hopefully it's as thrilling to watch as it is to perform."

Once the first season was a boffo hit, Benedict suddenly realized he was a star. Next up were major roles in Steven Spielberg's *War Horse*, *Star Trek Into Darkness*, the BBC miniseries *Parade's End*, the Best Picture Oscar–winner *12 Years a Slave*, *The Fifth Estate*, and *The Hobbit*, playing Smaug to Martin Freeman's Bilbo Baggins. He sang in *August: Osage County* and even voiced Severus Snape in an episode of *The Simpsons*.

But he didn't leave the theater behind. Before Jonny Lee Miller started making his own deductions as Sherlock

Holmes, he and Benedict took on roles in a unique production of *Frankenstein*, directed by Danny Boyle for the Royal National Theatre. From February to May 2011, the two men shared the two main roles, with Cumberbatch playing the Creature one night while Miller played Victor Frankenstein, and then switching the following night. The show was such a critical smash that the National Theatre broadcast two of the March performances live to Cineplex Odeon theaters around the world, followed by encore screenings in 2012 and 2014. Both actors are extraordinary, with Cumberbatch playing the Creature as a man who could once walk and talk and must now relearn how to do both, and Miller playing his Creature as a child learning to do both for the first time. The two shared the Best Actor trophy at the Olivier Awards and London Evening Standard Theatre Awards, and Cumberbatch took home the same award on his own at the Critics' Circle Theatre Awards; in doing so, he accomplished what is called the "Triple Crown of London Theater."

It wasn't just theater awards he was being nominated for: he racked up nominations for television (*Sherlock*, *Parade's End*) — winning an Emmy in 2014 for his role as Holmes — and film, receiving BAFTA noms for *Tinker Tailor Soldier Spy* and *The Imitation Game*, and being nominated twice in the same category for his parts in the ensembles of *August: Osage County* and *12 Years a Slave*. He's been awarded in all three media in which he works, but he and Freeman still joke about getting a Retrafta one day: "It's something Martin and I made up. Where you act so badly, they come and take your BAFTA off you."

In interviews Cumberbatch can be fiery and doesn't suffer fools gladly — he's told more than one critic to go home to do his homework — and his strong political beliefs and impatience for tabloids led to some controversy on the set of *Sherlock* when he was filming the third season. In the midst of working on the third episode, where his character appeared to be strung out, he was walking to his car in costume when a paparazzo snapped a photo of him. He walked over and asked if the guy could delete the photo, explaining that publishing it could be a major plot spoiler for fans. The photographer refused, so Cumberbatch pulled the gray hoodie over his head and continued his walk while holding up a sign that read, "Go photograph Egypt and show the world something important." The British press — where tabloid newspapers and magazines far outnumber broadsheets — had a field day, so Cumberbatch held up more signs later in the shoot, commenting on democracy and national security, asking such questions as "Is this erosion of civil liberties winning the war on terror . . . ?" The press could mock him all they wanted, but one thing was for certain: this was *not* a stupid actor.

Despite having a lot to say, Cumberbatch shies away from social media. He's famously verbose — many interviewers comment on his very long responses to their questions, and any attempt to interrupt simply makes him turn up the volume and keep right on talking — and for that reason he eschews Twitter. Someone who not only wants to make a statement, but explain that statement because he's studied every area of the topic, doesn't belong in a 140-character universe. "I get on with my work and my fans are very respectful of that, weirdly," he says. "I think they'd love it if I started Tweeting, but as I've said before, the people who are good at it are great at it. It's like a new art form. It's phenomenal how much it's opened channels of communication. I like those channels of communication for my work, but I don't want to journalize my life and publicize it because I really value my privacy and also my time."

He's still trying to get used to his stardom, which, despite all his years as a working actor, has come on quite suddenly. He still rides his motorbike and takes the Tube when he needs to, but he's no longer anonymous. "The strange thing is walking into a room and knowing that people recognize you," he says, "and you don't know who they are. That's a different energy that you have to get used to, and some days I'm good at that and some days I'm not. And when I'm not I feel self-conscious. But I still plow on with my day. I don't scuttle home. I don't want to live in a world where I have to build high walls."

With stardom comes the inevitable fan adoration and loss of privacy, especially regarding his romantic life. While at the University of Manchester, he met fellow actor Olivia Poulet, best known from *In the Thick of It*, a sharply written and bitingly hilarious British political comic drama. The two of them dated for 11 years, amicably splitting in 2011. Cumberbatch dated a few other women, and his half-sister even suggested to the media that perhaps he was so intelligent it made finding an equal match rather difficult. In several interviews he talked about how badly he wanted to settle down and start a family, and how much he loved children and wanted to have some of his own some day. "My mother's daughter from her first marriage had a kid when I was about 11," he recalls. "I thought, 'Wow, this is incredible, they come in much smaller sizes!' I was only used to my band of brothers at prep school. I was always the one at parties who looked after the younger children. I really enjoyed it."

On the fifth of November, 2014 ("Remember, remember..."), the internet exploded when a very simple notice appeared in the *Times'* Forthcoming Marriages column: "Mr B.T. Cumberbatch and Miss S.I. Hunter. The engagement is announced between Benedict, son of Wanda and Timothy Cumberbatch of London, and Sophie, daughter of Katharine Hunter of Edinburgh and Charles Hunter of London." Sophie Hunter, an actress, writer, and theater director, became one of the most-searched names on the internet that day as some fans took to Twitter to express their deep sorrow at the announcement, while others were overjoyed. Somehow he'd managed to keep the relationship itself pretty quiet and under wraps — they met on the set of the 2009 film *Burlesque Fairytales* — and the announcement came as a shock to some people. On January 7, 2015, the internet crashed once again with the news that Cumberbatch and Hunter were expecting a Cumberbaby later that year. The day after Cumberbatch received the prestigious Commander of the Order of the British Empire honor from the queen, his son arrived on June 13, 2015.

With season four of *Sherlock* — among countless other projects — on the horizon, Benedict's star continues to skyrocket. He has just become a father, secured Oscar and Golden Globe nominations for *The Imitation Game*, and was even named Britain's dishiest actor by a national British poll conducted by U.K. TV ... an honor that came with its own life-sized statue of Benedict made of 500 Belgian chocolates and weighing 88 pounds.

And frankly, I'd take that over an Oscar any day.

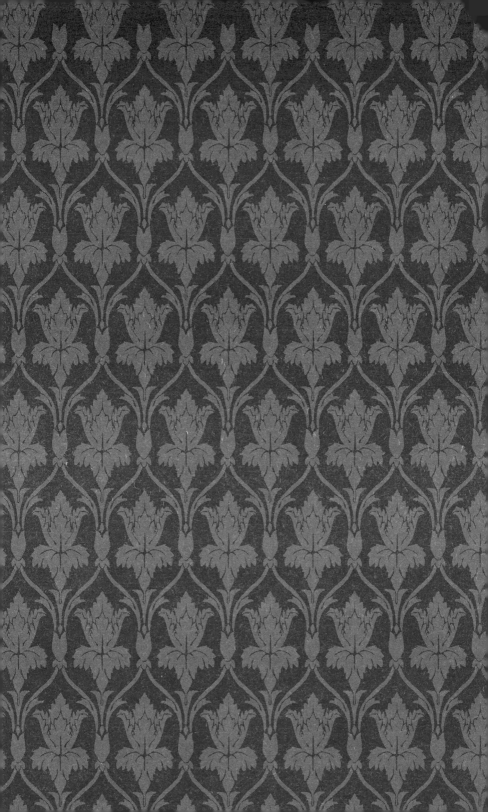

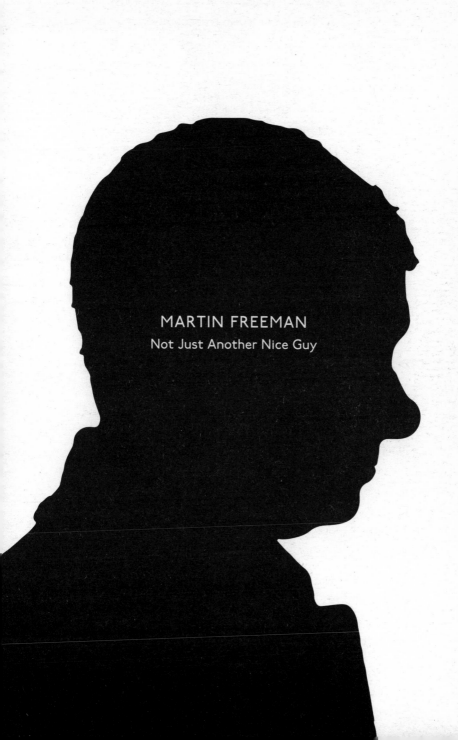

MARTIN FREEMAN
Not Just Another Nice Guy

When one reads various interviews with Martin Freeman over the years, one thing immediately becomes apparent: being thought of as "the nice guy" is Freeman's single biggest pet peeve. It doesn't sound like an insult at first, but the constant barrage of "nice guy" / "everyman" / "just playing himself" comments over the years have piled up. The responses he gives from the early to mid-2000s feature tons of swearing, as if he's trying to show what a nice guy he is *not*; in the late 2000s he cuts back on the crudeness (perhaps fatherhood mellowed that side of him) but snaps if one tries to broach his private life; and more recent interviews are a mix of the two, with him remaining staunchly close-lipped on the nature of his relationship with his partner Amanda Abbington (Mary Watson on *Sherlock*) while losing his mind if the interviewer refers to him as an everyman.

But given the sheer range in his performances over the years, plumbing the depths of joy and sadness — no other actor can manage the stilted, stuttering flurry of emotion that Freeman has accomplished on more than one occasion on *Sherlock* — one can't exactly blame him. While Cumberbatch was the choice for Sherlock all along, it took Freeman in the role of John for the creators to know they had a magical combination on their hands.

Freeman was born in Aldershot on September 8, 1971, the youngest of five children after Benedict, Laura, Jamie, and Tim. His parents, Geoffrey and Philomena, divorced when he was still a toddler, and Martin went to live with his father, a naval officer. His dad died suddenly of a heart attack when Martin was 10, and the boy returned to live with his mother. "My dad's death was no picnic," he says, "but, when I was younger, I was hell-bent on not looking bothered by it." A quiet child who suffered from asthma and what he calls a "dodgy leg," Freeman was nonetheless athletic, playing football and squash; he played on the British national squash squad between the ages of 9 and 14.

Though he joined a theater troupe at age 15, he didn't decide to become an actor until two years later. "When I was 17, I acted in a play called *The Roses of Eyam*, about a Derbyshire village during the Great Plague of 1666. I remember thinking I was doing quite well. It was the first time I got a lot of really positive feedback for my acting — the first time I had real confidence in myself. Acting, for me, feels like an absolute expression — a really necessary one." He attended the Central School of Speech and Drama, and after graduation it wasn't long before he was getting roles in both television and film. The most important role was in the TV movie *Men Only*, where he met Amanda Abbington.

His big break came in 2001 when he was cast as Tim Canterbury on Ricky Gervais's groundbreaking comedy *The Office*. Soon viewers all over the U.K. — and across the ocean — were swooning over Tim and Dawn, watching Freeman's trademark reactions to the antics of David Brent, Gareth, and "Big Keith." Overnight he went from a character actor to an instantly recognizable star, but being readily identified with one specific part had a major disadvantage: the nice-guy typecasting. Before Tim, Martin could play businessmen, rapists, pimps, even a beat-boxing thug in *Ali G Indahouse*. But now, for all intents and purposes, in the public imagination, he was Tim Canterbury, all-round nice guy. The series wrapped in 2003, and he was already starting to get sick of it.

"When people call me an everyman they think it's a compliment," he told the *London Evening Standard*. "I want to rip their f****** eyeballs out." As his fame grew from taking parts like Arthur Dent in *The Hitchhiker's Guide to the Galaxy* or Bilbo

Baggins in *The Hobbit*, the you're-just-playing-yourself misperception grew as well.

"Well, no I'm not," he told the *Guardian* in 2009. "If you mean I look a bit like him and I sound a bit like him — yeah, that's because I'm playing him and it didn't say 'He's Somalian' on the script, otherwise I would have tried an accent. If the script says, 'Guy in his 30s, my generation, lives in England,' what am I going to do? Start acting like I'm half-lizard? There's no point, because no one wants to see it."

In 2014, when he was cast in the brilliant television series *Fargo* playing the unfortunate Lester Nygaard, he was faced with the question once again. "I don't think other actors are asked all the time about the similarities between their roles," he said. "I don't think Ben [Cumberbatch] or Daniel Craig are asked that. I think it stems from my so-called perceived approachability . . . I'm a good actor; I can pretend."

Dear journalists: please stop asking him this question.

After *The Office*, Freeman gave a critically acclaimed performance in *Love Actually* as a stand-in body double who's shyly trying to ask the actress he's fake-banging on film out on a date. He also appeared in the first two movies in Simon Pegg's Cornetto Trilogy — *Shaun of the Dead* and *Hot Fuzz* — and starred in the final one, *The World's End* (which may have been an inspiration for John Watson's stag night on *Sherlock*). He's won a BAFTA and an Emmy for his role as John Watson, as well an Emmy nom for *Fargo*, and his lead role in *The Hobbit* has made him an international superstar.

Benedict Cumberbatch, for one, is very aware of Freeman's astonishing talents. "He's extraordinary," he says. "I honestly felt myself get better as an actor playing scenes opposite him — he has a brilliant level of humanity. We all know how funny he can be from his work on *The Office*, but he can also play so much pathos — it's an unsung talent of his that's often clouded by his *Office* fame."

One thing that drew Freeman to *Sherlock* was that he saw it as the perfect mix of comedy and drama, which is usually a marker of the best shows. "There is great comedy in *The Sopranos*," he says, "and there is great pathos in *Laurel and Hardy*. I think because, with comedy, the reason I like doing [*Sherlock*], it's not a new toy for me where I really want to flex that muscle and be funny. There are great funny moments in *Sherlock* but my instinct, especially because people think I am funny, is to always play against it and get rid of laughs. I like being straight. I want variation. I want to have my cake and eat it. Even in *The Office*, which I think is extremely funny, I was playing the straight man. Ricky Gervais's David Brent gets most of the quotes. I don't believe in hogging — the story has to be in charge."

As his fame grew, Freeman, like his *Sherlock* co-star, valued his personal life even more. He and Abbington have two children, and when he tired of fans ringing his North London doorbell at all hours hoping "Tim" would open the door, the two of them moved out of the city. Despite being offered bigger and bigger roles, he often hesitates if he thinks the job will take him away from his family for long periods of time. "My main priority in any job is when is the soonest I can get back to the three people I love most in the world," he says. "I even ummed and ahhed over *The Hobbit*." While he readily admits to being a grump, he's also a very hands-on father when he's at home. "It goes without saying that you're going to love your kids, but what you're not expecting is wanting to kill everybody in your house," he jokes. "I'm fortunate in that Amanda is generally a slightly nicer person than I am. If it were purely up to me, my kids would probably be vegetarian Catholic Marxists."

When the second season of *Sherlock* was airing, Freeman and Abbington joined Steven Moffat and Mark Gatiss at Gatiss's house to watch "The Hounds of Baskerville." Afterwards they asked Abbington to come out to the kitchen to discuss the part of Mary. She thought they wanted her advice, and then they told her they wanted it to be her. "I probably got quite emotional at that point," she says. But the opportunity to work with her husband, thus meaning more time together, was irresistible. "I think Martin and I bounce off each other very well. He is one of my favorite actors. He's so easy to work with and so creative. He brings something different to every single take. He is so on top of his lines that he can dig down and find a different angle every time. That really keeps you on your toes. Both characters go on a wonderful journey, and to do that with Martin was such fun."

Her main hope for the character was not to be a third wheel to Sherlock and John, but instead to complement their relationship. "Ben and Martin have real chemistry, and I had to hold my own in the scenes with them," she says. "It was daunting — not necessarily to come between them, but to arrive as another dynamic." As soon as Mary told John she liked Sherlock, the fans knew they'd have very little to worry about.

One of the first scenes they shot that season was where Sherlock revealed himself to John in the restaurant. "It was slightly surreal," says Abbington, "because it did feel like he'd been away, and [John] hadn't seen him. It was so charged, that scene. When John sees Sherlock for the first time, and then looks at Mary, it's that look of 'I don't know what I'm going to do now.' Both Martin and Ben pitched it so beautifully, especially Martin. In that one look, you see those two years of hurt. It was heartbreaking."

While Freeman plays coy with the are-they-or-aren't-they-married aspect of their real-life relationship, Abbington is clear that they aren't, and that it was very strange to film the wedding episode of *Sherlock* when they hadn't actually had one themselves. "Maybe one day we will," she says. "It sometimes does [come up], 'Should we do it?' I think we will, eventually. Our children are saying now, 'Mummy, you should get married.' They know we're not. Especially my son, who's going, 'Please, Mama, please be married.' Maybe we'll do it in Italy."

A self-declared homebody who likes to stay in and listen to music or watch a movie on DVD with his family, Freeman is one of the cool kids who prefers the comforts of home to the wildness of international stardom. "Some people have that roar in their head, but I'm not sure I ever did," he says. "That live-fast-die-young thing. No one wants it really — Jimi Hendrix, Janis Joplin — it's not good. I want to live with Amanda till I'm 70."

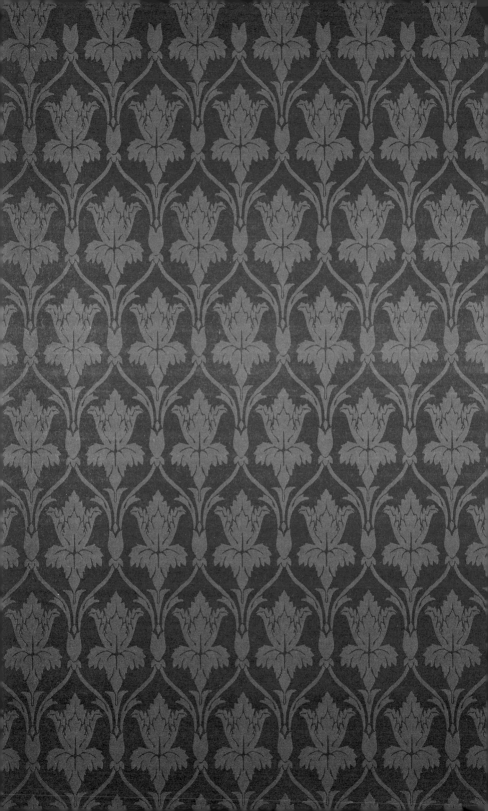

SIR ARTHUR CONAN DOYLE

The Father of Sherlock Holmes

To truly wrap your head around BBC's *Sherlock*, one must go to the source material written by Sir Arthur Conan Doyle. Mark Gatiss and Steven Moffat are such Doyle fanboys (they've been reading the books since they were in short pants), it's often astonishing to find all of the little nods the writers slip into the individual scripts.

Born in 1859 in Edinburgh, Doyle was enrolled in a prep school by age nine, and being away at boarding school meant a treasure trove of letters home to his mother, Mary, whom he referred to as "the Mam." These letters, finally opened to the public in 1997 by the Doyle family, offer extraordinary insight into the complicated man who's as fascinating as the detective he created. Doyle studied to become a medical doctor, and at the University of Edinburgh Medical School he met the larger-than-life Joseph Bell, a professor who had a huge impact on Doyle's life. At 39 years old, Bell was still rather young, but he was, according to Doyle biographer Russell Miller, "already a legend among medical students as a master of observation, logic, and deduction, possessing almost clairvoyant powers of diagnosis." Bell taught the students how to diagnose a patient without asking them a single question, instead simply observing the patient and concluding from those observations what might be wrong. He believed that while the patient could provide information that was invisible to the doctor, there was a wealth of information available if one only observed properly. He used a trick in class to emphasize the importance of noticing small details: he passed around a container of horrible-tasting liquid, asking the students to stick their fingers in it and taste it. In the name of fairness, he did it first, which forced each student to do it after him. Only after the container made its way throughout the classroom, much to the discomfort of each student's tongue, did he confess that he had stuck his index finger into the container but sucked on his middle finger. If they'd only paid close attention, they would have saved their tastebuds the horrible experience they'd just undergone.

Bell's methods stuck with Doyle, and after he graduated he opened his own practice in Southsea. He began publishing fiction on the side, and in 1885 he married Louise Hawkins (whom he referred to as Touie). Two years later, Touie wrote to Doyle's sister Lottie, "Arthur has written another book, a little novel about 200 pages long, called *A Study in Scarlet*. It went off last night."

Doyle had long been a fan of the work of Émile Gaboriau, known as a pioneer of modern detective fiction, and Edgar Allan Poe's Chevalier Dupin, and had longed to create a detective character of his own. He wrote in his memoir, "I thought of my old teacher Joe Bell, of his eagle face, of his curious ways, of his eerie trick of spotting details. If he were a detective he would surely reduce this fascinating but unorganised business to something nearer to an exact science . . ." It was in this characterization of Joseph Bell that Doyle hit upon what would set his detective fiction apart from everything that had come before it: Sherlock Holmes would, according to Miller, "solve his cases by pure deduction and not, as was commonplace in popular detective fiction, because of an absurdly convenient coincidence which, [Doyle] said, 'struck me as not a fair way of playing the game.'"

The first Sherlock Holmes novel was not an overnight success, even though it was a brilliant introduction to the character who was, as Orson Welles once put it, "the world's most famous man who never was." It was published in *Beeton's Christmas Annual* in 1887 for a one-time author fee of £25, with no ongoing royalties. (One can only imagine the income that Doyle and his heirs have lost in the years since its publication.)

Despite the tepid public reaction to *A Study in Scarlet*, Doyle published the second Holmes novel, *The Sign of Four*, in 1889, and in 1891 Holmes short stories began appearing in the *Strand*. Excellent reviews for *The Sign of Four* led to an increased readership, and the new enthusiasm and public demand for more stories led to Doyle closing his practice to become a full-time writer; he was making more money through the stories than he made in his practice. The paltry payment he'd been given for *A Study in Scarlet* is less difficult to accept when one realizes that by the turn of the century Doyle was the highest-paid author in the world.

Critics praised the ingenious storylines: Doyle could write about Mormonism, then switch to a story involving the Indian Mutiny and an evil pygmy dwarf who picks off his victims with a blowpipe. What audiences winced at, however, was the revelation in *The Sign of Four* that Holmes was a cocaine addict. At the time, cocaine was not perceived as being as nefarious as it is now; in fact, it was regularly used in hospitals as an anesthetic (along with heroin), and one could obtain it with little to no hassle. But still, according to Miller, "Some readers were appalled that a man of Sherlock Holmes's intellect and strength of character would inject himself with drugs, but Conan Doyle always wanted to distance his detective from the plodding image of a policeman: languid, bohemian, aesthetic, eccentric, Holmes viewed the science of criminal investigation as an art form and, as an artist, why should he not enjoy the pleasures of the needle?"

Doyle wrote each short story in under a week with almost no research (which accounts for the vast number of glaring inconsistencies between them). "A Scandal in Bohemia," where Holmes is faced with a woman as brilliant as he is and must try to stop a royal scandal, was a smash hit upon publication.

Doyle's editor, Herbert Greenhough Smith, described what it was like receiving the manuscripts for the first time: "Here, to an editor jaded with wading through reams of impossible stuff, comes a gift from Heaven, a godsend in the shape of the story that brought a gleam of happiness into the despairing life of this weary editor."

Doyle suggested to the *Strand* that they use Walter Paget, who worked with several magazines at the time, for the Holmes illustrations, but the art director couldn't recall his first name, so he simply sent the request to "Mr. Paget." It fell into the hands of Walter's brother Sidney, who took the job. Illustrating the story "Silver Blaze" (which ultimately became the first story in the second collection, *The Memoirs of Sherlock Holmes*), Paget drew the detective in a deerstalker hat and a long cape, which have now become synonymous with Sherlock Holmes (despite the fact that Doyle never mentions either accoutrement in the stories).

By 1892, people were lining up at the newsagents waiting for a new story to come out, and Doyle was baffled and annoyed. He had wanted Sherlock Holmes to be a one-off character, not one that he would have to continue writing about for the rest of his life. *A Study in Scarlet* was written over a three-week period when Doyle was 27 years old, and by the time he was in his early 30s, he wanted to be finished with the great detective so he could focus on his science fiction and historical fiction. In a letter to his mother, he revealed that he'd decided to kill the character, and despite her pleading with him not to, he began working on that final story. In a letter in 1893 he wrote to her, "I am in the middle of the last Holmes Story, after which the gentleman vanishes, never never to reappear. I am weary of his name."

And so, later that year, he killed off his greatest character in a fight to the death with the evil Professor Moriarty (a mathematician, a career choice inspired by Doyle having detested mathematics as a boy), as both of them tumbled over the great Reichenbach Falls in "The Final Problem." The story was published just before Christmas, and readers were devastated and went into mourning, some young men going so far as to wear black crepe mourning bands on their hats or arms. For Doyle's part, he simply wrote in his journal, "Killed Holmes."

The detective was dead, and Doyle tried to move on with his life and his writing. His father, who had been a severe alcoholic and was institutionalized at the time, died, and then Doyle's wife, Touie, contracted tuberculosis. Doyle began traveling, first becoming a war correspondent in Egypt, then in South Africa during the Boer War. Upon his return, he published some historical novels and continued to take care of his wife as she battled TB.

In 1897, he met and fell in love with another woman, Jean Leckie, but both vowed that despite their love, they would not act upon it until Touie had died. (Neither one of them could have foreseen that Touie was going to hang on for another nine years.) Leckie became a regular visitor at the home and got to know Doyle's two children, Mary and Kingsley. Doyle's letters to his mother during this long period express his passion for Jean, his love and devotion to Touie, his frustration at the situation, and even some regret. It's unclear if Touie knew about Doyle and Jean's true feelings for each other, though it's likely she did.

In 1899, actor William Gillette portrayed Sherlock Holmes for the first time on the London stage. The play, written by Gillette with the approval and aid of Doyle, was an overnight success. Doyle had been hesitant at first, and turned down previous suggestions of putting Holmes onstage. "I am well convinced," he wrote in the early 1890s, "that Holmes is not fitted for dramatic representation. His reasonings and deductions (which are the whole point of the character) would become an intolerable bore upon the stage." The very first time Doyle met Gillette, however, Gillette stepped off the train in a cape and deerstalker, and began to deduce that Arthur Conan Doyle was indeed the famous writer of the Sherlock Holmes stories. Doyle was instantly charmed, and Gillette looked exactly the way Doyle had always pictured Holmes in his head.

Unfortunately for Doyle, the success of the play led to a renewed clarion call for new Sherlock Holmes stories. Doyle had long been fascinated by the supernatural and had an idea for a story about a terrifying hound on the moors. By reshaping the idea into a Sherlock Holmes novel (but, for the most part, actually removing Holmes from the action and having Watson do the detective work), he created a sensation when he published *The Hound of the Baskervilles*, about an heir to the Baskerville mansion and the family legend of a hound that kills members of the family. The plot takes place in 1889, before Holmes had "died." The public was overjoyed that Holmes had returned, and Doyle decided he had to bring the detective back. Doyle was knighted, and a year later Sherlock returned to the land of the living in "The Adventure of the Empty House," dressing up as an old bookseller and scaring his dear friend Watson into a dead faint when he revealed himself to be Watson's long-dead friend.

One thing that dogged Doyle was the fact that the public seemed to think that he *was* Sherlock Holmes. When he showed up to readings he noted that audiences looked let down when he didn't look like Holmes at all. He wrote angrily in one of his letters, "I learned afterwards that they expected to see in me a cadaverous-looking person with marks of cocaine injections all over him." And yet, in 1906, Doyle was called in on a particularly difficult case for Scotland Yard, where a young man, George Edalji, had been charged with killing cows in his neighborhood. Doyle excitedly accepted the task, and successfully proved that Edalji did *not*, in fact, kill the cows, and that he had been set up and the case was more likely racism at work.

Later that year, Touie succumbed to tuberculosis. Despite having loved Leckie for as long as he had, Doyle was still devastated when his beloved wife died; the fact that she lived for 13 years after her diagnosis is a testament to how well he had taken care of her. However, upon his marriage to Leckie in 1907, Doyle immediately shipped both of his children off to boarding school, and surviving letters from his daughter, Mary, to his son, Kingsley, suggest that Doyle was treating them heartlessly as he moved on with Leckie, devoting himself to his wife and not even letting the children come home for holidays. Between 1909 and 1912, Doyle and Leckie had three more children, which pushed Mary and Kingsley even further out of the picture.

In 1912, Doyle published *The Lost World*, his most famous work outside the Holmes canon, and the reviews were very positive. Doyle was still writing Holmes stories at the same time — seven stories written between 1908 and 1917 comprise his fourth short-story collection, and *The Valley of Fear*, the fourth and final Holmes novel, was serialized from 1914 to 1915. But he was keen to write material outside of detective fiction.

When the First World War broke out in 1914, Doyle formed a volunteer force and was a tireless fundraiser for the soldiers, and his writing at the time reflects this involvement in the war effort. When his son Kingsley died of influenza a mere two weeks before the Armistice that ended the war, Doyle was beside himself.

During the war, Doyle became involved with spiritualism, and he and Leckie toured the world spreading the word of this cult. They held regular séances in their house, and Doyle sincerely thought he was bringing comfort to people who had lost loved ones in the war by encouraging the bereaved to contact the spirit world. Some people thought the Doyles were frauds, others believed they were just misled, and still others believed wholeheartedly in what they were doing. On one particular trip to the U.S., Doyle met up with Harry Houdini, who challenged him to make him a believer in spiritualism, claiming that spiritualists are simply using magic tricks. While Doyle was unable to convince him, the two men remained friends.

However, many other prominent figures in letters were starting to distance themselves from the great writer, believing that his devotion to spiritualism hinted that he had lost his mind. T.S. Eliot referred to Doyle's "mental decay," and P.G. Wodehouse suggested that Doyle had "simply fallen victim to hubris."

Just before the end of the war, two little girls from Cottingley in northern England took photographs of fairies they had seen in the woods, with the little creatures dancing in trees and sitting on the girls' hands. Despite the fact that the fairies were cut out from a popular children's book, which should have tipped off most people, and stuck to the trees with hatpins, the public fell for the ruse. Doyle was called up to take a look at the photographs, and he declared them authentic in the *Strand* in 1920 and 1921; they formed the basis for his book *The Coming of the Fairies* in 1922. It wasn't until 1985 — 55 years after Doyle's death — that one of the girls finally admitted publicly that the photographs had been faked. She said that it was Doyle's involvement that forced the girls to maintain their fiction, because she didn't want to embarrass him.

Doyle devoted most of the rest of his life to touring the U.S., Australia, Canada, and South Africa to promote spiritualism, publishing books on the subject. He continued to write prolifically outside of the Holmes canon — in all he wrote 23 novels, almost 180 short stories, 17 books of non-fiction, and seven stage plays, including one libretto with J.M. Barrie — and his final collection of Sherlock Holmes stories was published in 1927.

Sir Arthur Conan Doyle died in July 1930 at the age of 71, and within 24 hours his family members reported having received messages from him from the other side. He "appeared" at his own funeral dressed in his evening clothes (according to a medium that was present) and his wife insisted that she received messages from him until her death in 1940.

Regardless of what anyone thinks of his beliefs later in life, and much to the chagrin of the author beyond the grave, Doyle will always be remembered for Sherlock Holmes, the detective who taught the world not just to look, but to *observe*.

SHERLOCK

Episode Guide

The following is a complete guide to the three seasons of *Sherlock*. Each guide analyzes the episodes overall, before moving into the following sections:

HIGHLIGHT This is something funny that happened in the episode that was worth noting.

DID YOU NOTICE? These are little hints at future episodes, or things happening in the background that viewers may have missed.

FROM ACD TO BBC A list of all of the references to the original Sir Arthur Conan Doyle canon that were adapted to the BBC series. I'll use "Holmes" and "Watson" to refer to Doyle's characters, and "Sherlock" and "John" for the characters on *Sherlock*.

INTERESTING FACTS Behind the scenes information, or explanations of certain things alluded to in the episode but not fully elaborated upon.

NITPICKS Little things that annoyed me when I was watching but that could perhaps be explained away.

OOPS Outright bloopers or mistakes.

BENEDICT CUMBERBATCH as Sherlock Holmes

MARTIN FREEMAN as John Watson

MARK GATISS as Mycroft Holmes

RUPERT GRAVES as DI Lestrade

UNA STUBBS as Mrs. Hudson

LOUISE BREALEY as Molly Hooper

VINETTE ROBINSON as Sgt. Sally Donovan

JONATHAN ARIS as Philip Anderson

ANDREW SCOTT as Jim Moriarty

AMANDA ABBINGTON as Mary Morstan

SEASON ONE (2010)
Dr. Watson, Meet Mr. Holmes

The first season of *Sherlock* is about the early stages of one of the greatest pairings in all of literature: the friendship of Sherlock Holmes and Dr. John Watson. In the original 60 stories, with only three exceptions, the entire characterization and voice of Holmes is filtered through the pen of Watson. On more than one occasion, Holmes complains about Watson romanticizing of their adventures together, arguing that Watson's careful crafting creates a specific story, whereas in the hands of another writer the tale would be very different. Watson's writing is often self-deprecating, setting up Holmes as the superior mind and himself as the guy who's just along for the ride. In many subsequent adaptations, the depiction has been exactly that — Holmes as the calm, careful genius, with the bumbling Watson by his side sticking up for him every step of the way.

But a careful reading of the stories shows something very different. Watson is often annoyed by Holmes. In *The Valley of Fear*, he refers to himself as "one of the most long-suffering of mortals." When Holmes lies to him in *The Hound of the Baskervilles*, Watson is very upset, and he bitterly tells Holmes that he's wasted his time and shown nothing but distrust of him. There are more subtle hints as well, as when Watson describes Holmes in unseemly ways, pointing out his sexism or quoting deplorable comments, as if these are his tiny acts of revenge for having to put up with a friend who, at times, can be a bit of a dick. Holmes might mock Watson on occasion, pointing out his mental inferiority (and, again, Watson includes this information in the stories as if only to point out the boorishness of his pal), but Holmes values Watson, opens up to him in ways he doesn't to anyone else, is calmed by him, and when Watson's life is in danger, Holmes shows more fear than at any other time. A careful reading, like the one Steven Moffat and Mark Gatiss would have done, shows the intimacy between these two men — that they are not a genius and bumbling sidekick, but two men on an adventure, side by side.

From the momentous meeting of the two men in "A Study in Pink" to John saving Sherlock's life at the end of the episode, to the two helping each other solve the case in "A Blind Banker," to facing death together at the end of "The Great Game," this first season evolves their relationship from its birth to its maturity, the moment where Sherlock realizes that John is as important to him as he is to John. John pulls Sherlock out of solitude and makes him less of a social outcast, and Sherlock puts the danger and excitement back into John's life, which is exactly what John needed. Sherlock has the mind of a genius, but John has the social skills and humanity that Sherlock lacks.

This is not the story of a great detective and his sidekick, but of two men: John Watson, a man who is missing something in his life and who finds it in Sherlock Holmes, a man who doesn't realize he needed someone until he finds John. Ultimately, over the first three seasons, the show's focus will shift to Sherlock as we see his various strengths and flaws reflected in his foes, but John will always be there, shaping the man that Sherlock becomes.

A STUDY IN PINK

WRITTEN BY Steven Moffat

DIRECTED BY Paul McGuigan

ORIGINAL AIR DATE July 25, 2010

Sherlock and John meet for the first time and immediately begin investigating a series of suicides that Sherlock believes to be serial murders.

It's one of the most famous first encounters in literature, when the army doctor meets the world's first "consulting detective," who deduces his life story at first glance. When Dr. John Watson, home from the war, runs into his old friend Mike Stamford at the Criterion bar, Mike tells him about a friend of his looking for a flatmate, a man who "is a little queer in his ideas," Mike says carefully, and perhaps "a little scientific for my tastes — it approaches to cold-bloodedness," but overall he's "a decent fellow enough." And with that ringing endorsement, Watson prepares to meet the great detective himself, Sherlock Holmes. He walks into a lab in St. Bart's Hospital, where Holmes has just successfully found a way to prove when blood is at the scene of a crime (something that hadn't actually been done at the time) and is hopping about in excitement. He turns to greet Watson, extending a hand and saying, "You have been in Afghanistan, I perceive," and then proceeds to tell him how he knew that. A legendary friendship is born.

According to Gatiss and Moffat, no other adaptation has actually shown this momentous meeting between Holmes and Watson, despite Watson describing it in *A Study in Scarlet* in some detail. Instead, previous adaptations lead audiences into thinking that Watson and Holmes have always known each other. But for the *Sherlock* creators, it was important to first show the two separately and then bring them together, because the main theme of the first season was how each man's life is saved and changed by the other.

"A Study in Pink" opens with images of rapid gunfire, frantic shouting, groups of soldiers running in a whirl of confusion. John Watson sits up in bed, gasping for breath before falling back onto his pillow, turning to his side, and sobbing. Quiet, sad piano chords strengthen our impression that this man is very lonely, traumatized by the war, and consumed by his memories of it.

Sherlock, on the other hand, doesn't make an appearance until eight minutes in, and the first shot of him is upside-down, opening a body bag. We peer straight up from the bag as he stares down at us, sniffing the air and asking, "How fresh?" Molly Hooper stands near to him, telling him that the dead man used to be a colleague of hers. He stands up, quickly zips up the bag, turns to her with a fake smile, and says, "Right. We'll start with the riding crop." Upbeat gypsy music plays as we cut to Sherlock straddling the corpse and beating it mercilessly as Molly looks on, wincing.

What a huge contrast between the introductions of the two key characters: John's is full of sadness and loneliness; Sherlock's is humorous. We identify with John more readily because Sherlock comes across as so alien. John is depicted in a spartan, dark bedroom; Sherlock is in a fluorescently lit mortuary. John is all alone and runs into an old friend; Sherlock is with a colleague who has a crush on him but he barely notices she's there, let alone picks up on her feelings.

When the two men finally do meet up, it's a glorious scene.

Unlike his literary counterpart, this Sherlock doesn't notice John any more than he did Molly. He's not leaping about excitedly, but quietly staring through a microscope as if unable or unwilling to speak to anyone at that moment. John simply stands awkwardly in the corner of the room, leaning on his cane and looking uncomfortable. Mike Stamford sits nearby with a smile on his face, waiting for the show to start, and when it does Sherlock does not disappoint.

"Afghanistan or Iraq?" he says to John, who looks stunned by the question. John's bafflement continues throughout the scene for, unlike the Stamford of the book who graciously prepared Watson for his first meeting with Holmes, this Stamford seems amused by John being unnerved. John is a man who is lonely yet unsure of how to integrate back into society, and Sherlock is a man happy to be on his own, yet needs a flatmate. They are thrown together, rather than actually wanting to be friends, and it's only when Sherlock asks John to join him on a case that the real action begins.

This episode is based on the first Sherlock Holmes story, a novel called *A Study in Scarlet* (1887). Split into two parts, it first recounts the original meeting between Sherlock Holmes (who describes himself as a consulting detective) and Dr. John Watson, and their first case together: a man has been murdered, a wedding band has been found at the scene, and during the course of their investigation a second man is murdered. Despite the evidence pointing to other suspects, Holmes triumphantly announces at the end of part one that he has caught the murderer: Jefferson Hope, a cab driver who had been driven by revenge (*rache*) to track down the two men who had murdered the woman he loved back in America. The book then shifts in part two to the American Midwest several years earlier, and a long story involving kidnapping, murder, and Mormonism.

Critics often dismiss the second part, which explains that the devout Latter-Day Saints tried to force Jefferson Hope into polygamous relationships and then threatened to kidnap the one woman he loved so she could marry the group leader, leading to his avowed revenge on the men who perpetrated it. However, despite Doyle being a little loose with the details of Mormonism, the accusations the story lobs against the Church of Latter-Day Saints — namely its treatment of women — is an issue that still continues today; the story almost seems ahead of its time. Despite moving away from Baker Street and onto the American frontier, it is still a rip-roaring story full of suspense and intrigue, returning us to Holmes and Watson only at the very end, as Jefferson Hope finally explains how he tracked down the murderous men who'd ruined his life.

Steven Moffat plays with the story, managing to include key components but changing enough of it to keep even the most ardent Sherlock Holmes fan guessing. The way he uses details of Doyle's work but alters their significance will be one of the key trademarks of the show — stay loyal to the source material, but give the longtime Holmes fans something new. The wedding band that was essential in the book becomes a detail on the corpse of the woman dressed in pink. When Anderson, the smarmy forensics guy who despises Sherlock, suggests that the word *RACHE* etched in the ground could be German for "revenge," Sherlock mocks him and says of course it's not, it's the beginning of the word "Rachel." In the book, Lestrade suggests the word could be short for Rachel, and Holmes informs him sarcastically, "'*Rache*' is the German for 'revenge'; so don't lose your time looking for Miss Rachel." (It seems that no matter what century we place him in, Holmes will contradict the suppositions of the police force.) At the scene of the crime, Sherlock deduces the story behind the victim; his literary counterpart deduces who the killer is. The pills remain the same — in the book we are told that "of the two pills in that box, one was of the most deadly poison, and the other was entirely harmless" — but Jefferson Hope doesn't just randomly kill people for money, he's committing crimes of passion.

The scenes of Sherlock's deductions are brilliantly done, both by showing the words flashing across the screen to give us a tiny insight into Sherlock's mind palace, and through Benedict Cumberbatch's extraordinarily fast delivery of his lines. The astounding conclusions he comes to about John simply by looking at his mobile phone, and his work at the scene of a crime alongside the perplexed Lestrade utterly astonish his new friend. Some of the deductions might be considered a little silly, but if we suspend our disbelief and just enjoy the moment, the quickness with which Sherlock takes in the scene and identifies major clues that any other person would have missed, and then presents his findings with magnificent drama, renders the other characters and the viewers at home simultaneously gobsmacked and delighted.

But Sherlock is far from perfect. When he leaves John all alone and rushes away from the crime scene (so used to working solo he inconsiderately forgets all about his new companion), the sad piano chords and the lonely look on John's face (and Sally Donovan's words of caution) make us wonder if Sherlock, though fun to watch, isn't exactly best friend material. Sherlock's changeability and untrustworthiness are cornerstones of his character in the episodes to come, and the doubt that both Mycroft and Sally attempt to put in John's mind is purposefully made plain in this first episode: a man who seems to know *too* much might be hiding something.

Mycroft Holmes is a character who appears only twice in the books, and is bordering on obese, so the tall, slim Mark Gatiss

him and see him as inhuman, cold, insensitive, and arrogant, basking in the awe of those around him and caring more for his deductions than behaving like a human being. But the reason we like him is because John does. Martin Freeman is perfection as John Watson, a flawless portrayal of a man whose deepest fear is loneliness, who is awed by Sherlock's mind yet unafraid to call out Sherlock when he acts like an ass. Much to Sherlock's surprise, the detective's growing friendship and appreciation of John forces him to care about someone other than himself for once. And, as Sherlock will discover time and again, caring for someone else can be as much of a danger as a comfort.

The writing and direction of this episode are superb, and Moffat and Gatiss recognize that there is a lot of humor to be mined from Doyle's books. Sherlock's pithy comebacks to both Anderson and Donovan, or his reaction to John turning down Mycroft's offer to pay him to spy on Sherlock — "We could have split the fee. Think it through next time" — or the way Sherlock and John walk away from the crime scene at the end, giggling like two schoolboys . . . all of these moments demonstrate that this will be a show that knows how to combine humor with drama. There are the ongoing "are they gay?" jokes, from Mrs. Hudson insisting she's okay with it and that Mrs. Turner next door even has "married ones," to Angelo, the restaurant owner, assuming Sherlock's on a date (and ignoring their insistence that they're not by bringing out a romantic candle), to John awkwardly trying to find out if Sherlock's in a relationship and Sherlock mistaking his general interest for a romantic one. Moffat and Gatiss both know that over the years there has been some serious speculation and scholarship surrounding the possible romantic relationship between the two men, and decide to attempt to nip it in the bud right away by making it a joke. (Of course, as any fan knows, the shippers watching the show who *want* the relationship to be there will find it anyway — as they did with Xena and Gabrielle — and the Johnlock fanfic is alive and well.)

At the end of the episode, as John and Sherlock leave the crime scene after the younger Holmes reveals Mycroft's identity — "You can *imagine* the Christmas dinners" — their friendship has already grown in leaps and bounds, and they are no longer two individuals, but a team.

HIGHLIGHT

Sherlock: Why have I got this blanket? They keep putting this blanket on me.
Lestrade: Yeah, it's for shock.
Sherlock: I'm not *in* shock.
Lestrade: Yeah, but some of the guys want to take photographs.

DID YOU NOTICE?

- Throughout the series, there is a gorgeous, plaintive piano melody consisting of four chords (Am, D9/A, Gm, F/C) that's called "Watson's Theme." Present at moments when John is alone or sad, it always serves to take a scene that's already full of pathos (due to the brilliance of Martin Freeman) and make it even more heartbreaking. In this episode, it's the first music we hear, in the scene following John's dream as we see him alone in his apartment. It plays again when John comes out of the crime scene he visited with Sherlock to find that his flatmate has departed without him, when

Mycroft reminds him of the life he had before Sherlock, when Sherlock takes the taxi and leaves John at the apartment, in the taxi on the way over to where Jeff is with Sherlock, and finally when he's running through the halls of the building looking for Sherlock. In each instance, the sad chord progression indicates John's fear of the banal, lonely existence he had before he met the dynamic Sherlock Holmes. Listen for it at key moments throughout this season.

- John's mug says *"In Arduis Fidelis,"* which translates to "Faithful in adversity." Not only is it the motto of the British Army, but it also proves relevant to his relationship with Sherlock.

- When John opens his desk drawer at the beginning of the episode, we glimpse a gun inside. It's the same revolver that he shoots at the end of the episode, adhering to Chekhov's principle, which states that a playwright should never introduce a gun on stage unless he intends for it to go off at some point during the play.

- In the U.K., there are many opponents to the vast number of CCTV cameras, who liken them to Big Brother in George Orwell's *1984*. In a sly wink to that, the cameras in *Sherlock* are actually being controlled by Sherlock's big brother.

FROM ACD TO BBC Aside from what was mentioned already, there are other small details from *A Study in Scarlet*:

- After running into Mike Stamford, John joins him at a bar called the Criterion. In this episode, "Criterion" is written on John's coffee cup.

- We see Sherlock beating a body with a riding crop to see how quickly bruises form; in the story, Stamford says he's heard of Holmes beating dead bodies to see how quickly bruises form.

- Sherlock's blog is called "The Science of Deduction," which is the title of chapters in both *A Study in Scarlet* and *The Sign of Four*.

- At one point in the novel, Watson notices that Holmes has a vacant, dreamy stare, and says, "I might have suspected him of being addicted to the use of some narcotic, had not the temperance and cleanliness of his whole life forbidden such a notion." Similarly, John refuses to entertain the thought that Sherlock may have been a junkie.

- When John and Sherlock catch up to the cab, they discover its passenger is innocent: he's simply an American visiting London for the first time. In the novel, Jefferson Hope is the American visiting London for the first time.

- When Holmes realizes that the murderer drives a cab, he says a line very similar to that of Sherlock's on the show: "supposing one man wished to dog another through London, what better means could he adopt than to turn cabdriver?"

- Jefferson Hope suffers from an aortic aneurysm, whereas Jeff Hope has a brain aneurysm.

The description of Holmes in the books is quite similar to the physical attributes of Sherlock on the show: "In height he was rather over six feet, and so excessively lean that he seemed to be considerably taller. His eyes were sharp and piercing, save during those intervals of torpor to which I have alluded; and his thin, hawk-like nose gave his whole expression an air of alertness and decision."

The second victim is James Phillimore, who runs home in the rain to get his umbrella and never returns. In "The Problem of Thor Bridge," when Watson is listing off their unsolved cases, he says, "Among these unfinished tales is that of Mr. James Phillimore, who, stepping back into his own house to get his umbrella, was never more seen in this world."

Sherlock asks to borrow Mike's phone, saying he prefers to text rather than make a call. In the books, Holmes famously sends telegrams everywhere, long after telephones were widely used.

When Sherlock finds out about the fourth murder, he shouts with excitement and says, "Oh, it's Christmas!" In *The Valley of Fear*, Watson describes the look of delight on his friend's face right after an announcement that someone had been murdered: "It was one of those dramatic moments for which my friend existed . . . Without having a tinge of cruelty in his singular composition, he was undoubtedly callous from long overstimulation."

Sherlock deduces a lot of information about John based on his cellphone. In *The Sign of Four*, Watson hands Holmes his watch, and Holmes comes to similar conclusions — that the watch belonged to his brother who was an alcoholic, that their relationship was a stormy one, etc. Watson is very upset at first, thinking that Holmes had made inquiries into his past, until Holmes explains how he figured it out. In the books, Harry is indeed Watson's brother, not a nickname for his sister, Harriet.

One of the many inconsistencies in the Sherlock Holmes stories is where Watson's war wound is actually located. In *A Study in Scarlet*, he says quite specifically that he was honorably discharged from the war because of a wound in his shoulder. However, in later stories the wound mysteriously travels to his leg. Some fans have speculated that the shot was another magic bullet à la *JFK*, which entered his shoulder, ricocheted off something, and then came back through his leg. Gatiss and Moffat pay homage to Doyle's inconsistency by first having John walk with a cane for a leg injury, which is determined to be psychosomatic, and only at the end of the episode does John reveal he was actually wounded in the shoulder.

Another inconsistency in the canon is the name of the landlady: first, she is Mrs. Hudson. Then, in a couple of stories, she becomes Mrs. Turner. Then Doyle returns to Mrs. Hudson. As a nod to the inconsistency, Mrs. Hudson refers to a Mrs. Turner, the next-door neighbor who is also a landlady. Amusingly, the joke carries over to John Watson's blog (JohnWatsonBlog .co.uk), which is run by the BBC, where there are often comments left by "Marie Turner," who, as she reveals in later comments, is actually Mrs. Hudson borrowing Mrs. Turner's laptop.

Sherlock's declaration — "The game, Mrs. Hudson, is *on!*" — is a reworking of Holmes's famous, oft-repeated pronouncement, "The game is afoot!"

Mycroft Holmes is introduced in "The Greek Interpreter" as "absolutely corpulent," with a massive face, which is why there are several jokes in upcoming episodes about him being on a diet. In "The Adventure of the Bruce-Partington Plans," Watson says of Mycroft that "after the first glance one forgot the gross body and remembered only the dominant mind."

Sherlock's texts to John as John is meeting Mycroft for the first time — "Come at once if convenient"; "If inconvenient, come anyway" — are taken from a telegram that Holmes sends to Watson in one of the final stories, "The Adventure of the Creeping Man."

John discovers early on that at times he's no more important than an inanimate object, and that Sherlock doesn't even notice if he leaves a room. In "The Adventure of the Creeping Man," Watson says this was his role in Holmes's life in the later years: "He liked to think aloud in my presence. His remarks could hardly be said to be made to me — many of them would have been as appropriately addressed to his bedstead — but none the less, having formed the habit, it has become in some way helpful that I should register and interject."

Sherlock referring to the case as a "three-patch problem" is a reference to the "three-pipe problem" he faces in "The Red-Headed League." The look of euphoria on Sherlock's face as he slaps on the last patch matches Holmes's expression when he injects cocaine in front of Watson in *The Sign of Four*.

The idea that John is a man attracted to danger is certainly part of the stories. In one example, from "The Adventure of the Three Garridebs," Holmes tells Watson that he knows Watson will want to accompany him on a particular case simply because it involves danger, and adds, "I should know my Watson by now."

Jeff tells Sherlock, "You are just a man. And there is so much more than that. An organization." This echoes Professor Moriarty's statement to Holmes in "The Final Problem": "You stand in the way not merely of an individual but of a mighty organization, the full extent of which you, with all your cleverness, have been unable to realize."

At the end of the episode, Sherlock begins deducing who could have shot Jeff Hope when he suddenly realizes it was John, and he tells Lestrade to forget everything. In "The Adventure of Charles Augustus Milverton," Holmes and Watson break into Milverton's place to help cover up a crime that happens when they're there. When Lestrade tells Holmes that two men were seen at Milverton's place and describes one of them to him, Holmes laughs, "That's rather vague. My, it might be a description of Watson!"

At the end of the episode, Mycroft says he has a "minor position" in the British government, to which Sherlock replies, "He *is* the British government." In the stories when Holmes describes his brother to Watson, he says, "You are right in thinking that he is under the British government. You would also be right in a sense if you said that occasionally he *is* the British government."

INTERESTING FACTS

- The scene of John and Sherlock chasing the cab driver through the streets of London begins in Soho and is filmed on many London streets, but when they finally catch up to the cab, they're in Cardiff.
- Phil Davis, who plays Jeff, was unable to be on set the day the drugs bust scene was filmed in the Cardiff 221B set, so another actor played his character when he appears in the doorway. That's why the camera simply zooms in on the pink phone in his pocket and his face is in the shadows.

NITPICKS If Sherlock had already moved into the flat, why doesn't Mrs. Hudson look surprised when he knocks on the front door and waits to be let in?

OOPS Sherlock and John agree to meet at 221B Baker Street to check out the flat at 7 o'clock the following evening. However, when they meet there, it's clearly mid-day.

It's something that has irked scientists and linguists for decades: Sherlock Holmes does not solve crimes through *deductions*, but *inductions*. However, in every adaptation since Doyle, the incorrect word has been used, including on *Sherlock*. So what is the difference between deduction and induction?

According to science humorist Dave Zobel in his book *The Science of TV's The Big Bang Theory*, "Deductive reasoning begins with a collection of statements known to be true." These aren't guesses, but known facts put together to reach a conclusion that is infallible; in other words, there's no way this conclusion could be incorrect. Induction, on the other hand, is based on observations where the observer then uses "pattern matching, hunches, and intuition to try to guess at a rule that accounts for those observations." These conclusions could be proven false if the guess is wrong. It's like in a game of Clue: players propose a solution when they've seen enough evidence to make an educated guess, but until one knows every single card one's opponents are holding, one cannot know for certain which three cards are hidden in that envelope.

Let's look at Sherlock's "deductions" in "A Study in Pink." When he's investigating the corpse of the woman, he says her marriage is falling apart because the inside of her wedding ring is shiny but the outside is tarnished, as if she pulls it off regularly for a string of affairs but doesn't bother polishing it. Her coat collar is slightly damp, the umbrella unused, which means she's been in rain-soaked Cardiff and the wind prevented the umbrella from being opened. Are those indisputable conclusions? Of course not: perhaps she takes the wedding ring off each night because she doesn't like sleeping with it on; perhaps she washed her coat and it wasn't completely dry when she had to put it on; perhaps the button on her umbrella didn't work and she was unable to open it. Sherlock's observations lead him to certain plausible conclusions, but those conclusions are never infallible. In Doyle's books, there are several instances where Holmes offers up his "deductions," and they turn out to be wrong.

Sherlock is better at observing and making educated guesses than anyone else, but *deduction* doesn't even come into it. That said, for the purposes of matching what is said on the show, throughout this book I use the term deduction (with a wince) to describe what he does.

THE BLIND BANKER

WRITTEN BY Steve Thompson
DIRECTED BY Euros Lyn
ORIGINAL AIR DATE August 1, 2010

As John gets back into the workforce and the dating scene, Sherlock takes a case for an old friend involving mysterious yellow ciphers.

In our second outing with Sherlock and John, we see the new friendship as it develops . . . and we also see the tiny cracks beginning to appear. John has already discovered that the adventurous life promised as Sherlock's companion comes at a price — a price that the ATM card reader won't let him pay. Without a job, and relying on Sherlock, John decides to find a sort of independence within this codependent relationship.

Sherlock, on the other hand, continues to have conversations with the air, not noticing that John has actually left the room.

Where "A Study in Pink" used characters and storylines from the Sherlock Holmes stories to introduce the world of 221B Baker Street to viewers, "The Blind Banker" — the only episode this season not written by Moffat or Gatiss — moves away from canon (while occasionally dipping into it) and focuses more on the two central characters. Even Lestrade is absent, as another inspector, the remarkably young DI Dimmock, steps in to deal with Sherlock on a case. Where Lestrade explained in the previous episode that he uses Sherlock when he's desperate, and because he truly believes that Sherlock is a good man, Dimmock very reluctantly deals with Sherlock, ignoring and dismissing his theories until Sherlock has to jump through several hoops to prove he might be on to something.

One key aspect that sets the 21st-century *Sherlock* apart from the world of Holmes's gaslights and hansom cabs is its commentary on modern-day anti-intellectualism. In Doyle's novels, as in many of the adaptations, Holmes's genius is something that is upheld by others, who are wonderstruck as he presents his solutions at the end of each case with a flourish. Watson admires him so much that he devotes his life to chronicling the extraordinary adventures of the man, while his clients often speculate that Holmes has something of the supernatural about him to be able to deduce so much from so little. Only the detectives are occasionally annoyed by him in the books, but that's only because Holmes's deductions usually unveil their own inferiorities as investigators. There are several instances where the detectives openly say that they couldn't solve half the cases without Holmes's help, and in one case — "The Disappearance of Lady Frances Carfax" — Holmes and Watson are caught doing something illegal, but when the police are called in, they immediately let Holmes go out of respect.

On *Sherlock*, however, the detective's intelligence is something to be mocked. While John and even Lestrade are in awe of what Sherlock does, Sally Donovan refers to him as "the freak," Dimmock dismisses him as being a lunatic, and Anderson acts like he's a pox on the police force. In this episode, we see that this treatment actually bothers Sherlock. When he and John are called out to the bank to investigate a strange cipher that has been graffitied onto a painting, Sherlock is greeted by an old friend, Sebastian, and Sherlock asks him about flying around the world twice in a month. John has started to get used to Sherlock's "thing," as Sebastian then puts it, and snickers as Sebastian teases Sherlock about his "trick."

"We were at uni together," he says to John, as if Sherlock isn't even in the room. "This guy here had a trick he used to do . . . We hated him." While Sebastian continues to mock him, asking if perhaps there's some ketchup on his shirt or mud on his shoes that Sherlock noticed, Sherlock looks uncomfortable. He turns away, shuffles in his seat, stares at the floor, and begins muttering that it's not a trick, that he just observed. Finally, he looks at Sebastian and says, "I was just chatting with your secretary outside." We later discover that, in fact, he had looked at Sebastian's watch when he shook his hand, but in this moment, to escape Sebastian's contempt, to try to appear *normal*, he lies and acts like he'd gotten his information the way ordinary people would have done.

It's this utter disdain that everyone else has for him that sets the early 21st century apart from the late 19th: Arthur Conan Doyle's character lived in a society that would have been awed by his intellectual prowess. But today, in a world where irony is the overriding tone and stupidity the overriding element — the highest-rated shows seem to celebrate the lowest IQs — Sherlock isn't someone to be upheld but to be sneered at, which is a very interesting element Gatiss and Moffat have added that says a lot about our era and anyone who values knowledge above all else.

One of co-creator Steven Moffat's strengths (and occasionally a weakness) is his penchant for looking into the psychology of his characters, as he's done on *Doctor Who*. So it was natural for him to take an iconic literary character and do the same thing: what must it be like for someone as intelligent as Sherlock Holmes to travel in the circles of the common folk? To be so uncommonly gifted with the powers of observation, to see things that other people miss, to have to explain what to him seems patently obvious? To always feel like the smartest person in the room? By introducing Mycroft as a more prominent character, one whose derision for his little brother has nothing to do with Sherlock's intelligence (since he thinks his brother is a moron compared to himself) but more with everyday sibling rivalry, Moffat and Gatiss spotlight Sherlock as a person rather than a peculiar character.

And so, that little moment of pain that passes over Sherlock's face as he sits in Sebastian's office is much more important than it might at first seem. It's a tiny glimpse into the difficult world Sherlock inhabits. Perhaps the reason he comes off as cold and isolated is because that's the way he likes it: better to push people away than to try to fit in and be the butt of everyone's jokes. He's made an attempt to escape society and friendships; it's John who will pull him back in.

John, on the other hand, has found comfort and adventure in living with Sherlock, and now seeks to spread his wings into the greater world. The adventure is fun, but once he does away with his loneliness, he wants to live life to its fullest. To Sherlock, the cases *are* what life is all about: who needs money and romance when there are ciphers to be decoded?! Because John's time is limited, however, he conveniently combines both by dating a work colleague. Zoe Telford is wonderful as Sarah, the woman who falls for John even though he falls asleep on the job, but their first date is a bit of a travesty. Not only does Sherlock show up as a third wheel, but she ends up attacking someone with a stick, going hungry, getting kidnapped, and watching her life flash before her eyes. Surprisingly, she's still around in the next episode (perhaps she, too, craves danger and adventure?) but not beyond that.

Poor John. When the sad strains of "Watson's Theme" begin playing as Sarah stares down an arrow aimed at her head, we know what he's thinking: maybe he *is* destined to be alone in love. His craving for adventure might cost him any sort of life outside that adventure. It's one thing to long for danger; it's quite another to see a loved one facing danger because of you.

As Sherlock and John try to find their places within their new friendship, the case itself takes center stage . . . and that's where the main problems of this episode lie. For a series that tried to eschew Victorian trappings, it certainly holds fast to them here when it comes to racial stereotyping.

It begins with the opening of the written script, where Soo Lin Yao is described as "Pale, young, beautiful — a fragile little doll," immediately stripping her of any sort of strength or heroism on her own part; we know she's destined to be a victim. Despite the musical motifs of the show (the theme song, "Watson's Theme," and the "Hero's Theme" that plays when Sherlock is triumphant) all being derived from the same chord structure, in this scene we hear stereotypical "Oriental" music that is completely out of tune with the show's soundtrack, immediately denoting the ancient tea ceremony — and Soo Lin herself — as foreign and Other. Similarly, Arabian music plays during the scene of Sherlock fighting the Sikh man who bizarrely wields a samurai sword rather than a kirpan or ancient Sikh sword, loses the battle to an unarmed Sherlock, and is a mere footnote to the episode. When Sherlock and Watson travel to the Lucky Cat shop (a Chinese shop that inexplicably features several Japanese tchotchkes on its shelves), Chinatown is filmed differently than the rest of London. Gone are the fast-moving cars and people quickly walking by: now the music turns creepy, the alleyways shot like we're in the seamy underbelly of the city, where people lurk in doorways like criminals watching you with evil intent, or slink by eerily and slowly as if they have nothing better to do all day than be disconcerting and threatening. While Soo Lin is sympathetic, and her brother is portrayed as a puppet doing bad things against his will, the other Chinese characters are all criminals. Even the Chinese opera feels wrong — an ancient and beautiful Chinese tradition being used to mask something dark and sinister. There's an episode of *Doctor Who* from 1977 called "The Talons of Weng-Chiang" that is often cited as a favorite among fans for its excellent storytelling, but it's difficult to watch now because of its problematic depiction of Chinese people all belonging to the Tong gang (and the fact that the main character was played by a Caucasian actor in Fu Manchu makeup). That episode aired 33 years before this one, and it's the racist stereotypes that have dated it. How is it possible that three decades later the BBC would be committing the same error in judgment, right down to making the Chinese characters belong to none other than a Tong gang?

However, "The Blind Banker" still has some brilliant gems sprinkled throughout, from the excitement of Sherlock and John trying to decipher the codes, to the suspense of the escapology act, to the constant pile-up of evidence that John might actually be Sherlock Holmes, to that hilarious moment of Sherlock in "disguise" as a guy who's just forgotten his key and buzzes another tenant to let him into the building. The performances of Freeman and Cumberbatch save this episode and keep fans coming back to rewatch it again and again.

That said, when compared to "A Study in Pink" and "The Great Game," this is easily the weakest outing of season one.

HIGHLIGHT That epic pen toss.

DID YOU NOTICE?

- After John has the argument with the chip-and-PIN machine at the supermarket, he mutters, "Keep it, keep it," and walks away. One assumes he's referring to the groceries, but since he doesn't actually take the card back when he leaves, apparently he was telling the machine to keep that also.

- When John and Sherlock go to the bank, they go to Tower 42. The number 42 is significant in pop culture because of its importance in Douglas Adams's *The Hitchhiker's Guide to the Galaxy*, wherein a computer has been working out the key to "The Answer to the Ultimate Question of Life, the Universe, and Everything" for several million years. The answer? Forty-two. Martin Freeman starred in the 2005 film adaptation of the book.

- When Sherlock goes to Eddie Van Coon's flat, you can see a stack of books sitting near the fireplace, many of which are a wink to the plot of this episode: P.J. Tracy's *Snow Blind*; Simon Singh's *Fermat's Last Theorem*; Dan Brown's *The Lost Symbol*; George Savage's *Porcelain through the Ages*; James Ellroy's *Blood's a Rover*; Veronica Chambers's *Kickboxing Geishas: How Modern Japanese Women Are Changing Their Nation*; Mohamed El-Erian's *When Markets Collide: Investment Strategies for the Age of Global Economic Change*; Judith Miller's *Miller's Antiques*; Edna Healey's *Coutts & Co 1692–1992: The Portrait of a Private Bank*; Paul Lunde's *The Secrets of Codes: Understanding the World of Hidden Messages*; and the *London A–Z Street Atlas*.

- We learn a lot of facts about John's career from the brief flash of his CV: he went to King Edward Grammar School in Chelmsford from 1994 to 1999, attended King's College in London to obtain his Intercalated BSc in Medical Sciences (Hons) from 1999 to 2001, then took his Bachelor of Medicine and Bachelor of Surgery at the same college from 2001 to 2004, and received further medical training from 2004 to 2006. In his profile, he says he is "a conscientious, reliable, and hardworking medical professional, pays attention to details, crusader of clinical governance, with excellent interpersonal and time management skills, seeking further training and experience in accident and emergency medicine while working towards a career in laparoscopic and bloodless surgery."
- Zhi Zhu's fingerprint is on the glass of the photo frame in Soo Lin's apartment, as if he removed his glove and touched the face of his baby sister out of regret for what he was about to do; similarly, just before he kills her, Soo Lin reaches out and cups his face in her hands.
- When Sherlock is trying to come up with the book that everyone would own, he goes to his bookshelf and pulls off three. The first two — the *Oxford English Dictionary* and the *Holy Bible* — are probably optimistic, and the third one is downright hilarious and baffling: *Syphilis and Local Contagious Disorders* by Berkeley Hill.

FROM ACD TO BBC Most of the Doyle allusions in this episode are from his final Sherlock Holmes novel, *The Valley of Fear*:
- Just as Sherlock realizes the letters correspond to words in a book, Holmes finds a cipher in the agony column and tells Watson, "It is clearly a reference to the words

in a page of some book. Until I am told which page and which book I am powerless."

- In trying to figure out which book everyone would own, Sherlock pulls three from his shelf, including the bible and a dictionary. In *The Valley of Fear*, Holmes asks Watson to solve the problem. Watson suggests three books, and Holmes discounts each guess: the bible (Holmes says there are too many editions for each person to have the same page numbers); Bradshaw (closest to the solution in "The Blind Banker," it was a travel book about railway journeys; Holmes says the language is "nervous and terse, but limited"); and a dictionary (which Holmes says would have the same problems as the bible). The correct answer turns out to be the almanac.

- Holmes uncovers a secret society called the Scowrers, which is like the Black Lotus in that it pulls people in against their wills and then threatens to kill them if they leave. The Scowrers tattoo their forearms rather than their feet and are referred to by one character as a "murder society." Like the Black Lotus, their reign of terror is solely for profit, and, like the Mafia, they even collect protection money from local businesses.

- *The Valley of Fear* takes place near the beginning of the Holmes / Watson relationship, when Professor Moriarty is still alive. Moriarty's right-hand man and chief sniper is named Sebastian Moran, so calling Sherlock's banker colleague "Sebastian" was a nice bit of trickery, making us assume he might be evil when, in fact, he's just a jerk.

The ciphers in the episode are a reference to hieroglyphic drawings in "The Adventure of the Dancing Men," in which a code warns a woman that someone is coming to kill her husband.

Sherlock handily beats the Sikh fighter in his apartment. There are several references to Holmes being a good fighter in the stories. In *The Sign of Four*, he encounters McMurdo, a boxer who remembers Holmes as the guy who gave him a cross-hit under the jaw. In "The Adventure of the Empty House," he explains that he and Moriarty had a fight to the death on the edge of the Reichenbach Falls and he won. In "The Adventure of the Solitary Cyclist," Sherlock engages in a fist-fight in the street with another man and wins. In "The Yellow Face," Watson comments that Holmes was "undoubtedly one of the finest boxers of his weight that I have ever seen." And in "The Naval Treaty," he catches a thief red-handed, who then tries to get away, but Holmes takes him down, receiving a gash on his knuckles as a result.

Sebastian tells John that everyone hated Sherlock in university. In "The 'Gloria Scott,'" Holmes mentions he only had one friend in college — Victor Trevor — and adds, "I was never a very sociable fellow."

In "The Adventure of Black Peter," Watson writes of Holmes, "I have seldom known him claim any large reward for his inestimable services." In this episode, John does his best to change that.

By looking around Van Coon's apartment, Sherlock deduces that he must have been left-handed. In "The Yellow Face," Holmes and Watson try to make conclusions about a client simply by looking at his pipe, and Holmes suggests he's left-handed based on how charred the left side of the pipe is.

In "The Adventure of the Blue Carbuncle," Holmes interviews people not by asking them direct questions but by making them contradict him, knowing that in their anger they will become competitive and give him far more information, just as he does with Mumford's wife in the junkyard.

- In order to execute the pen toss (where John throws the pen to Sherlock, who catches it despite looking in a different direction), Cumberbatch was looking into a mirror so he could see the pen coming. He nailed it on the first try, but there was a problem with the camera and they had to redo it. Three takes later, he caught it again.

- John angrily tells Sherlock that the police are giving him an ASBO: an anti-social behavior order.

- Van Coon's secretary, Amanda, is played by Cumberbatch's then-girlfriend, Olivia Poulet. At the time of filming this episode, she had been in a relationship with Benedict Cumberbatch for 11 years. They amicably split a year later.

- Sherlock says he has decided not to take the "Jaria Diamond" case, and that he's sent them a message instead. Presumably, he's referring to the Sikh man he was fighting with at the beginning of the episode. Though the script spells it "Jaria," the name could be referring to Jharia, India, a city known for its coal mining, where a fire has been burning in one of the mines since 1916 (when Arthur Conan Doyle was still writing Sherlock Holmes stories).

- When John and Sherlock first arrive at the bank office, Sherlock notes a clock that says the New York time is 7:45. Minutes later, Sherlock looks at Sebastian's watch, which reads 12:04. Some fans have pointed this out as an impossibility, since there should be a five-hour time difference between London and New York. However, if it had taken Sherlock and John a few minutes to be seen by Sebastian, then 12:04 would be reasonable. New York time and London time are usually five hours apart, but there is a two-week difference between Daylight Savings Time's ending in the U.S. and in the U.K. In other words, during that two-week period, the clocks are only four hours apart. In 2010, when this episode takes place, that period was from March 14 to March 28; David died on March 22, which puts this moment squarely within that range. Sebastian's watch is correct. The other clock, however, isn't (see "Oops").

- When Sherlock is talking to Molly about the disgusting cafeteria food at St. Bart's, he says, "This place is never going to trouble Egon Ronay, is it?" He's referring to the food critic who published a series of guides to British and Irish restaurants in the '50s and '60s. Ronay died three weeks before the premiere of this episode.

NITPICKS

- Sherlock deduces that Eddie Van Coon was left-handed based on how he used the implements in his apartment, and he concludes that a left-handed individual wouldn't have been able to shoot himself on the right side of the head. However, many eagle-eyed fans have pointed out that Martin Freeman is similarly left-handed, yet John always holds his revolver in his right hand. Is he holding it in his right hand to be truer to the books (Doyle's Watson is right-handed) or is it possible for someone to hold a gun in their non-dominant hand? I asked a friend who is a sport shooter, and she had this to say: "Yes, it is possible for lefties to shoot right-handed and vice versa. . . . Shooting ability has less to do with your dominant hand, and more to do with eye dominance." In other words, the hand a person dominantly uses isn't necessarily the one in which he or she would shoot a gun, and while Sherlock is correct in this instance, it is possible for Van Coon to have shot himself.

- With all of the books in Brian Lukis's flat, how did Sherlock find the one he happened to be carrying with him on the night of his murder? And do we really believe that Lukis saw the cipher on the back of the shelf and ran terrified from the library all the way home . . . but stopped at the front desk to properly check out the book from the library first? And how would the Black Lotus have known exactly which book he was going to take out?

- Sherlock refers to Hangzhou as an ancient Chinese dialect, but a dialect is spoken, not written. Hangzhou refers to the *written* system.

- In the cipher meant for Soo Lin's eyes, the 1 is at the top, the 15 underneath it, whereas the other ciphers had the 15 on the top. This would have given her a different message (i.e., instead of looking at the first word on page 15, she would have turned to the 15th word on page one).

- When Sherlock realizes the cipher can be read through the A–Z guidebook, he immediately flips to what is supposed to be page 15 but looks like it's about 50 pages into the book.

- Sherlock grabs the guidebook and begins deciphering the code. When he does so, he turns his back to the German tourists, which means he's facing the door to 221B Baker Street. So how is it that Zhi Zhu came to his apartment door, knocked John unconscious, and kidnapped both him and Sarah, presumably taking them out the front, while Sherlock stood there the whole time? It's clear the detective gets very involved in his work, but geez, Sherlock, what happened to your powers of observation?

- Two men pick up Sarah's chair and move it into the line of fire. So since the chair isn't bolted to the ground, why doesn't she flip her chair over to save herself the same way John did? It would have been nice to see her take matters into her own hands rather than being a damsel in distress who needs to be saved by Sherlock.
- Sherlock mentions that Chinese visas are scarce, and General Shan had to rely on someone with connections and wealth to obtain them for her circus troupe. However, a visa isn't difficult to obtain if one has enough money to pay for one, and with the money the Black Lotus gang has been making from selling Chinese antiques, one would think they'd have the cash.

OOPS

- Gemma Chan, who plays Soo Lin Yao, is a British actress who puts on a Chinese accent for the purpose of playing a Chinese refugee. However, it wavers, and many fans have been amused by the way she says "Is that security?" in the beginning of the episode without even a hint of the Chinese accent she uses elsewhere.
- While the time difference between Sebastian's watch and the clock is correct (see "Interesting Facts"), another clock is wrong. Upon arrival, Sherlock notices the New York time is 7:45. When he is in the offices probably half an hour later, the New York clock in that room reads 7:21.
- When Sherlock is at the bank offices, skipping and twirling around the room to figure out who could see the cipher from where they were sitting, he moves around one column and then brushes by another. The second one moves quite noticeably and is clearly a flimsy set decoration.

- Despite John's CV declaring that he has great attention to detail, he writes that he trained at the "University Collgege [sic] Hospital in London."
- When Sherlock finds Eddie's train ticket, the station is misspelled "Picadilly."
- General Shan tells Sherlock there aren't any blanks in the gun the second time, but there weren't any blanks in there the first time, either; blanks make a gunshot noise, and instead the gun just clicked, meaning the chamber was completely empty.
- Some viewers have taken issue with the fact that Sherlock refers to Shan's pistol as a semi-automatic, but it appears to be a Walther, which is indeed a semi. However, the bullets of a Walther travel at just over 1,000 *feet* per second, not meters, as Sherlock suggests.

SHERLOCKIANS WEIGH IN
Christopher Redmond

Christopher Redmond is investitured as Billy in the Baker Street Irregulars, the most exclusive Holmes society in the world, and is a member of the Bootmakers of Toronto and a number of other Sherlockian societies. He is the author of several books, including A Sherlock Holmes Handbook *(Dundurn Press, 2009), and is the administrator of Sherlockian.net.*

Do you think *Sherlock* is a faithful interpretation of the characters of Watson and Holmes?
I think it's a sincere attempt, particularly in the case of Holmes. Benedict Cumberbatch has the manic quality of the original Holmes (not so much the depressive states that go with it),

the brilliance and knowledge, the arrogance. He controls the arrogance less well than the original Holmes, who was somewhat constrained by Victorian standards of behavior, in spite of what we sometimes think. I don't think he has the aesthetic sensibility of the canonical Holmes, however.

As for Watson, my guess is that the creators of the series could not make themselves take a middle-class Victorian military gentleman (the original Watson) seriously. Thus they've had to imagine what an army doctor must be like, and in particular what psychological difficulties he must have in order to take up with the likes of a Sherlock Holmes. Watson's conventional wish for respectability and order gets overpowered by what the writers see as his pathological need for excitement. Maybe when he's as old as previous Watsons (not necessarily Nigel Bruce but, say, David Burke) he will be a bit more stable, a solid surface for Holmes to carom off.

What is your favorite aspect of Steven Moffat and Mark Gatiss's reimagining of the stories? What is your least favorite?

I am just delighted by the many reworkings of canonical details and plot points. My favorite, perhaps since it is the first one to surface in "A Study in Pink," is Sherlock's analysis of John's new cellphone, drawn wonderfully from his analysis of Watson's watch in *The Sign of Four*. The writers do this over and over. In the last episode (to date), "His Last Vow," I exclaimed happily in a tweet to Sherlockian friends: "Oh! Janine is Agatha!" It's a welcome way in which the scripts keep Sherlock and John's melodramatic personal lives at least slightly rooted in the original stories.

At the other extreme, I find the BBC's Moriarty just distasteful, some sort of lunatic whose interest lies entirely in his personality and his relationship with Holmes. The original Moriarty is a calm, businesslike schemer motivated by money — in fact very much like the Charles Augustus Magnussen of "His Last Vow" (though I realize that Magnussen is meant to be based on a different canonical figure altogether).

The BBC episodes rely far, far more than the original stories on investigating the personalities of Sherlock and John (and two or three figures around them) and seeing what happens when they are placed under stress in various combinations. I do not find this part of the story arc particularly interesting, and I disagree with those who think that it figures significantly in the Sherlock Holmes canon.

What has been your favorite adaptation of Doyle's stories so far?

I am entirely sold on the Granada Television episodes produced in the 1980s starring Jeremy Brett. Most of them keep as close to the canonical stories as they could possibly have done, not only in plot but in dialogue and even in the framing of many scenes to imitate the original Sidney Paget illustrations. Both of Brett's Watsons are brilliant, though I somewhat prefer the earlier, crisper David Burke to the later Edward Hardwicke.

Admittedly, they are middle-aged figures, perhaps better suited to the later Holmes stories than to the very early ones in which the detective and the doctor are necessarily young men. The BBC series took an interesting risk in making Holmes and Watson so young, and it seems to have been completely successful with young viewers, if perhaps not quite so successful with those of my generation.

A few of the later Granada episodes wander far from the original text and characters, and one or two of them include stream-of-consciousness scenes that are as uncongenial to me as the corresponding (and more frequent) scenes in BBC's *Sherlock*. Still, I'll watch most of Brett over and over again with continuing pleasure.

THE GREAT GAME

WRITTEN BY Mark Gatiss
DIRECTED BY Paul McGuigan
ORIGINAL AIR DATE August 8, 2010

In addition to trying to recover government plans for Mycroft, Sherlock and John are forced to solve several other mysteries within a certain time period to prevent further deaths. Sherlock finally meets his real arch-nemesis.

"The Great Game" is where *Sherlock* truly shines. The first episode was a brilliant introduction to the world of 221B Baker Street, and the second — while suffering from some racial issues — showed the development of the core relationship. But in this third installment, everything that has been built up over the previous three hours comes together: Sherlock's desperate need for action; John's questioning of who Sherlock really is; and the fine line separating those who solve crimes and those who commit them. All three storylines converge when we discover that Sherlock isn't the only genius who bores easily.

Despite only appearing in two Sherlock Holmes stories, Moriarty has gone down in history as one of the all-time great villains in literature. He has appeared as Holmes's foe in films, radio plays, stage productions, and television adaptations. He is, as Holmes says in the stories, "the Napoleon of evil."

Why are audiences so fascinated with this character if he's only in one story directly and another one indirectly? Because from the very moment he appears, Holmes regards him as his only intellectual equal. Like the ancient yin and yang symbols, Holmes and Moriarty aren't opposites but two parts of a complementary whole. Holmes is the consulting detective who is able to get into the mind of the criminal; Moriarty is the consulting criminal who wends his way into Holmes's mind.

Gatiss provides a masterful introduction to the evil genius through this fast-paced, intense episode that almost never stops being suspenseful. As Moriarty invites Sherlock to play his game — and Sherlock willingly accepts — we see the two brains pitted against one another, and yet working together. Moriarty continually praises Sherlock through his emissaries, and Sherlock eagerly dives into each case, becoming more impressed by his adversary. The fact that Moriarty has turned human beings into panic-stricken time bombs means nothing to the detective: for Sherlock, it's all about the game.

John, on the other hand, sees this as toying with people's lives and terrorizing them. He watches as his best friend gets pulled deeper and deeper into Moriarty's web, and his discomfort grows with Sherlock's delight. John tries to reason with Sherlock, but can't get through to him. Sherlock acts like he doesn't need John, and instead gives him some demeaning make-work tasks like sending him off to see Connie Prince's brother. John becomes convinced he's cracked the case . . . only to discover that Sherlock had solved it hours earlier, not only wasting John's time to get him out of the way but being utterly thoughtless about the distress he's causing the elderly blind woman who has C-4 explosives strapped to her.

By the time Sherlock gets to the pool at the end, one would think he doesn't have any humanity at all. When Molly Hooper introduces him to her boyfriend, "Jim," Sherlock's only comment is "gay," muttered under his breath. Of course, he has observations to back up that statement, but he knows better than to say it out loud, and does so anyway. When Moriarty's third time bomb agent doesn't follow protocol and Moriarty's sniper pulls the trigger, Sherlock puts the phone down, mouth open in surprise. The next morning, he and John realize just how horrible it was, that 11 people died in addition to the elderly woman. Sherlock sits quietly in the chair, devastated at the loss of human life. No, scratch that . . . he's upset that the explosion suggests that Moriarty won that round, when Sherlock knows that *he* won it because he had figured out the case in time. As he begins to piece together the three mysteries and what ties them together, John is infuriated: How could the two geniuses be playing with human beings this way? Don't they care about the lives at stake in their precious game? "Will caring about them help save them?" Sherlock asks.

It's a pertinent question. Surgeons don't weep over every patient they can't save. Veterinarians don't mourn the loss of every animal they have to euthanize. Soldiers can't stop to imagine the friends and families of the enemies they're shooting at. Sherlock is simply distancing himself from the human element because, as he will discover even more in the second season, when one begins to care it affects the outcome of the game. And the game is what matters to him. He needs to keep himself clear of human emotion and act more like a machine. It's that discipline that keeps his mind sharp, that ultimately gets the job done and puts the criminal element behind bars. He doesn't think of the people sitting in the car, or standing in Piccadilly Circus, or trapped in an apartment, covered in C-4 and crying for hours as they imagine their impending deaths. If he did, he wouldn't be entirely focused on the case; his concentration would be broken.

In contrast, watch how John investigates the case. He meets Connie Prince's brother, Kenny, and assumes he has a personal vendetta against his sister because of how strangely he acts. He imagines a wildly concocted scheme whereby the cat's claws are poisoned and he's able to take everything from his sister by killing her. John doesn't focus on the clues around him, but thinks of the way sibling relationships change over time (consider the damaged relationship between himself and Harry), and of how Connie treated Kenny in public, humiliating him over and over again. He's utterly wrong, of course, and Sherlock comes up with the more mundane solution, gleaned by simply observing the evidence and ignoring the possibilities of human drama. John's preference for romance over facts is illustrated in his blog posts, and Sherlock's abhorrence of John's versions of their investigations provides much of the hilarity of this episode. Sherlock mocks John for missing important clues, but John will always be able to counter that Sherlock *didn't know the Earth revolved around the sun.* Hard to beat that one, Sherlock.

Amid all the Moriarty-induced fun, Mycroft has returned to request Sherlock's assistance in helping him recover a memory stick that contains secret government plans that had been allegedly stolen by the now-deceased Andrew West. While Sherlock dismisses Mycroft's emphasis on the case's importance, John feels a responsibility to Sherlock's older brother and, under the guise of acting on behalf of Sherlock, takes on the case himself. Just as Sherlock sent him to Connie Prince's house knowing that John would be guided by his heart instead of his head, he similarly sends him to West's fiancée's house, knowing that John will do the requisite handholding and listening, paying attention to all of the emotions and none of the clues.

But best friends aren't supposed to be robots. John might miss essential clues during an investigation, but he cares about people, their fears and plights, and he worries about Sherlock. Sherlock's indifference to human suffering frustrates John constantly, and it's one thing to purse his lips and jab his finger in

Sherlock's direction as he lectures the sleuth about his apathy; it's quite another to live with him on a daily basis and slowly come to realize that Sherlock doesn't even notice his absence.

That's why the scene at the pool is essential to the entire season. Once again, Sherlock has gone behind John's back because of his obsession with the game. Moriarty instigated the game, but Sherlock is determined to win it. When John steps out of the shadows in a large coat and says, "Bet you never saw *this* coming," the look on Sherlock's face is priceless, matched only by the faces of the viewers at home wondering just how far Gatiss and Moffat have decided to veer from the books on *this* one. Sherlock is in shock — not, for once, because he can't believe he missed the clues leading up to this moment, but because he's so surprised that his best friend would betray him like this. A moment later, as John opens the coat to reveal the bombs, Sherlock's surprise turns to horror. Finally, here is a human being whose life he cares about. John begins muttering nonsense that's being fed to him by Moriarty, and Sherlock begs his enemy to stop. Not only does he want John to live, but he doesn't want him to be humiliated. From this point on, Sherlock seems to lack proper concentration and emotional distance and is instead focused on how he can save John's life. He's willing to turn over government secrets and — god forbid — forfeit the game, just to save his friend. He and John are more alike than either one could have guessed.

Moriarty finally steps out of the shadows, and . . . it's "Probably Gay" Jim from St. Bart's. "Hi," he sings in a high-pitched Irish lilt. Sherlock's face drops once again as he realizes that Moriarty had been under his nose the whole time. The intellectual limitations of everyone around him is a constant irritation for Sherlock. "You do see, you just don't *observe*," he hisses at Lestrade earlier in the episode. And yet, despite telling

Miss Wenceslas, "The art of disguise is knowing how to hide in plain sight," he had failed to observe that his arch-nemesis, the guy whom Sherlock paid no mind when he introduced himself earlier, the man who slipped his phone number under a petri dish . . . all along *he'd* been hiding in plain sight.

Throughout this episode, Benedict Cumberbatch is glorious, from his arrogant correction of a prisoner's grammar, to the way a smile threatens to dance on his lips when he realizes he's about to embark on a game, to the wide variety of emotions that play upon his face throughout this final scene. Martin Freeman is similarly remarkable as he tries to keep his anger in check around Sherlock, gets excited when he thinks he's cracked a case, attempts to sacrifice himself to save Sherlock's life, and then falls apart afterwards. Yet despite the mastery of these two actors, Andrew Scott as Moriarty is such a marvel you can't take your eyes off him. In this one scene, he's goofy, creepy, brilliant, terrifying, and hilarious, creating an entirely unsettling effect. As with Sherlock, the viewer knows when looking at Moriarty that he's a man devoid of empathy, but one who is an extraordinary actor who can make everyone around him do, say, and believe whatever he wants them to. He tricked Sherlock, and even as he walks around the pool, hands in his pockets, head bobbing from side to side, Sherlock can't quite figure him out. The master of detection and observation is stumped by this cunning person. Scott plays him as an extremely volatile man, one moment purring his words, the next shouting viciously. He speaks in a high, soft voice that almost lulls the listener into calmness. That tranquility suddenly disappears when Sherlock takes on John's moral high ground and reminds Moriarty that people have died because of their little game. "That's what people *DO!!*" Moriarty violently shouts, and his voice echoing around the pool area is chilling.

But Sherlock isn't the only one caught by surprise in this moment. Just when the detective seems to have run out of ideas, John leaps onto Moriarty's back and tells Sherlock to run. Moriarty isn't angered by this turn of events, but instead looks deeply impressed by both men. He knows that caring for a friend makes Sherlock weaker, but in this moment he admires that Sherlock has taken on a "pet" to help him out of difficult situations.

If there were ever a moment in this first season where we questioned Sherlock's loyalty to John, that doubt disappears when Moriarty leaves and Sherlock frantically removes the bomb vest from his friend. He looks upset and deeply shaken, repeatedly asking John if he's all right. He could have gone after Moriarty, but getting that vest off John is all that matters to him in this moment. When John asks Sherlock if he's okay, Sherlock simply dismisses the question with a wave and then begins to stutter out his thanks to John for doing what he did. This is probably the first time in Sherlock's life someone has thrown themselves in front of a bullet for him, has offered willingly to sacrifice his life to save Sherlock's, and the sleuth doesn't know how to process his new emotions. Notice when Moriarty walks back through the door — "I'm *so* changeable!" — and Sherlock points the gun at the bomb, he first looks to John, who gives him an almost imperceptible nod, as if they're now in this together, rather than Sherlock making the decisions and John having to live (or die) with them.

What happens next will make anyone watching the series for the first time thrilled that they aren't watching it live in August 2010 with a year and a half until the next episode.

John, on Sherlock's Homeless Network: "So . . . you scratch their backs, and . . ."
Sherlock: "Yes, then I disinfect myself."

DID YOU NOTICE?

- The yellow smiley face on the wall of Sherlock and John's flat has been made with the spray paint from the previous episode.
- The sign behind Moriarty when he's standing poolside cunningly hints that, until now, Sherlock has been paddling in the shallow end of the criminal pool.

FROM ACD TO BBC The memory stick portion of this episode is based heavily on "The Adventure of the Bruce-Partington Plans," a fantastic later story:

- The story begins with Holmes being incredibly bored, and he receives a notice from Mycroft that some very important government plans have been lost, and all of Britain would be compromised if they fell into the wrong hands. When he sends a telegram to Holmes saying he's coming over, Holmes is so shocked — his brother rarely leaves the safety of the Diogenes Club — that he remarks to Watson, "But that Mycroft should break out in this erratic fashion! A planet might as well leave its orbit."
- Although the sibling rivalry between Mycroft and Sherlock isn't nearly as heated in the stories as it is on the show, in this instance Mycroft tells Holmes, "You must drop everything, Sherlock. Never mind your usual petty puzzles of the police-court." In "The Greek Interpreter," the first time we encounter Mycroft, he

condescendingly refers to his brother as "my dear boy" (in the books, there's a seven-year age gap).

- When Mycroft tells Holmes that there's an honor in it for him, Holmes dismisses the offer and says, "I play the game for the game's sake," which ties this story into the rest of the episode.

- In the story, Arthur Cadogan West is framed with the robbery, killed, and thrown on top of a train, and when Watson visits with the fiancée she is as adamant as Andrew West's fiancée in the episode, saying, "Arthur was the most single-minded, chivalrous, patriotic man upon earth. He would have cut his right hand off before he would sell a State secret confided to his keeping. It is absurd, impossible, preposterous to anyone who knew him."

- At the end of "The Adventure of the Bruce-Partington Plans," Watson is scared about accompanying Holmes somewhere but agrees to go with him, and he notes, "For a moment I saw something in his eyes which was nearer to tenderness than I had ever seen." It's fitting that Sherlock would direct that same caring look to John at the end of this episode.

In "The Musgrave Ritual," Holmes is so bored he shoots "V.R." in the wall of the flat, which stands for Victoria Regina, just as he randomly shoots at Mrs. Hudson's wall in this episode.

Sherlock complains throughout the beginning of this episode that he is bored. In "The Red-Headed League," Holmes explains to Watson, "My life is spent in one long effort to escape from the commonplaces of existence. These little problems help me to do so."

There are several instances in the canon of Holmes criticizing Watson's storytelling, just as Sherlock mocks John's blog in this episode. At the beginning of *The Sign of Four*, Watson asks Holmes if he'd taken a look at his write-up of the previous adventure, *A Study in Scarlet*, and Holmes expresses the same sort of disdain for it as Sherlock does. "I glanced over it," he says. "Honestly, I cannot congratulate you upon it. Detection is, or ought to be, an exact science and should be treated in the same cold and unemotional manner. You have attempted to tinge it with romanticism, which produces much the same effect as if you worked a love-story or an elopement into the fifth proposition of Euclid." Watson expresses his displeasure to the reader, admitting, "I was annoyed at this criticism of a work which had been specially designed to please him. I confess, too, that I was irritated by the egotism which seemed to demand that every line of my pamphlet should be devoted to his own special doings." In "The Adventure of the Copper Beeches," Holmes goes so far as to suggest Watson embellishes the stories, and at first Watson good-naturedly ribs him back, until Holmes escalates the conversation by saying, "Crime is common. Logic is rare. Therefore it is upon the logic rather than upon the crime that you should dwell. You have degraded what should have been a course of lectures into a series of tales." Holmes says it again in "The Adventure of the Abbey Grange," adding, "I must admit, Watson, that you have some power of selection, which atones for much which I deplore in your narrative. Your fatal habit of looking at everything from the point of view of a story instead of as a scientific exercise has ruined what might have been an instructive and even classical series of demonstrations. You slur over work of the utmost finesse and delicacy, in order to dwell upon sensational details which may excite, but cannot possibly instruct, the reader."

John seems to take no end of pleasure in the fact that Sherlock knows very little about the solar system. In *A Study in Scarlet*, Watson writes that after living with Holmes for a short time, he'd made lists of things Holmes knew and things he didn't, and among the things he knows very little about are literature, philosophy, and politics. Watson adds that Holmes is "ignorant of the Copernican Theory and of the composition of the Solar System." Later, in *The Hound of the Baskervilles*, when Watson is a little ticked off with Holmes, he reminds him, "I can still remember your complete indifference as to whether the sun moved round the earth or the earth round the sun."

In "The Adventure of the Second Stain," a very important government document is stolen out of the bedroom lockbox of the Prime Minister's Secretary of European Affairs, the loss of which could start a war. Readers have often nitpicked that such an important document wouldn't just be put into a lockbox in someone's bedroom, but rather be kept in a safe in the Houses of Parliament. There is a sly nod to that story in this episode, when Mycroft explains that the plans for the missile defense system were being kept on a memory stick and John scoffs, "That wasn't very clever."

Sherlock asks John to find as many clues as he can on the shoe, and even though he doesn't come close to finding what Sherlock does, the detective praises him, only to then shoot down what he came up with. This is a running trope in the stories. In "The Adventure of the Missing Three-Quarter," Holmes asks for Watson's advice on their next step, and when Watson comes up with a plan, Holmes says, "Excellent, Watson! You are scintillating this evening," only to tell him he'd already thought of the plan, checked it out, and it wouldn't work. In "A Case of Identity," Holmes gives Watson the first shot at deducing a client, and after Watson's conclusions Holmes says, "'Pon my word, Watson, you are coming along wonderfully. You have really done very well indeed. It is true that you have missed everything of importance, but you have hit upon the method, and you have a quick eye for colour." At the beginning of *The Hound of the Baskervilles*, he has Watson make deductions about a cane that was left behind by a client, and Watson throws out a few ideas. Holmes begins to praise him exuberantly before adding, "I am afraid, my dear Watson, that most of your conclusions were erroneous."

John is upset to learn that while he thought he was being clever and working the case on his own (deducing that Connie Prince was somehow killed by the cat claws; starting to figure out that Andrew West's body was found where it was because of the train switches), Sherlock had been following him the entire time and had already cracked both cases. Sherlock's treatment of John is similar to the way he treats him in *The Hound of the Baskervilles*, when he sends Watson off to Baskerville on his own, and Watson sends back long reports to keep him abreast of events, only to discover that Holmes has been there the entire time, always keeping two steps ahead of Watson's investigation.

After Sherlock doesn't show appropriate concern in the wake of the elderly woman's death, John accuses of him being unfeeling. In *The Sign of Four*, during one particularly passionate outburst, Watson says to Holmes, "You really are an automaton — a calculating machine . . . There is something positively inhuman in you at times."

Moriarty is introduced (and then killed off) in Doyle's short story "The Final Problem." When Holmes tells Watson about him, he says, "If I could beat that man, if I could free society of him, I should feel that my own career had reached its summit, and I should be prepared to turn to some more placid line in life." When describing him, Holmes tells Watson that when their paths crossed, "I had at last met an antagonist who was my intellectual equal."

When Sherlock gets the first message from Moriarty, it's preceded by five pips. In Doyle's story "The Five Orange Pips," the title refers to members of the KKK sending messages to each other using dried-up orange seeds, or pips.

Sherlock tells John about his Homeless Network in this episode. In *The Sign of Four*, Holmes introduces Watson to the Baker Street Irregulars, a group of "street Arabs" who are able to inconspicuously gather information for Holmes far more effectively than the police force, simply because they're able to slip through the streets of London completely unnoticed.

Throughout this episode, Sherlock keeps saying that he needs more data. That was a word oft-used in the books: one prominent example is from "The Adventure of the Copper Beeches," when Holmes famously shouts, "Data! data! data! I can't make bricks without clay."

When Sherlock cracks the Bruce-Partington case, he tells John that Mycroft threatened him with a knighthood. At the beginning of "The Adventure of the Three Garridebs," Watson mentions that Holmes had just refused a knighthood.

When Moriarty and Holmes come face-to-face in "The Final Problem," Moriarty says, "All that I have to say has already crossed your mind." Holmes replies, "Then possibly my answer has crossed yours," dialogue that is echoed poolside in this episode. Moriarty is described as having a soft voice and is "clean-shaven, pale, and ascetic-looking."

Just as the flat across the street from theirs is blown up in this episode, 221B is set on fire in "The Final Problem."

INTERESTING FACTS

- Moffat and Gatiss say they chose Belarus as the setting for Sherlock lecturing the convict on his grammar for two reasons: they wanted it to be cold, and it's one of the only places in the world that still executes people by hanging. The scene was actually shot in Wales.

- For those outside the U.K., the Greenwich pips are a series of tones used by the BBC every 60 minutes to indicate the top of the hour. The series consists of six pips: five short, one long. The first time Sherlock is contacted by Moriarty, the message begins with five pips (four short, one long). In each subsequent phone call, the number of pips decreases by one.

- In the second case, Moriarty contacts Sherlock to tell him that the clue is in the name of the motor car company: Janus Cars. Janus is one of the oldest Roman gods and is depicted as having two faces: one looking forward to the future, and the other looking backward to the past. He was a good king who revered honesty above all other traits, but over time his allusions in literature, television, and film instead present a mistaken interpretation of his two faces. Janus now represents one who is two-faced, or hypocritical and deceitful (the opposite of what the god originally represented). So when Moriarty says his name is the clue, he's pointing to the fact that Janus Cars purports to be one thing, but in fact is deceiving the public by helping people disappear.

- Connie Prince's brother is played by John Sessions, whom North American audiences might recognize from the original British version of the popular game show *Whose Line Is It Anyway?*

- In the planetarium, the voice on the film Professor Kairns is watching belongs to *Doctor Who*'s fifth Doctor, Peter Davison. The music playing in the film clip is Gustav Holst's "Mars."

- The voice of the child on the phone during the Vermeer deduction is Louis Moffat, Steven Moffat's son. He will appear onscreen at the end of "His Last Vow."

- While there is no actual Van Buren supernova, Sherlock's solution to the mystery of the Vermeer painting has actually been used to date paintings. In 2013, a group of scientists at Texas State University used what is called "astronomical chronology" to date a series of Monet paintings; in one case, looking at a particular rock formation and the location in the sky of a sunset, they dated it to an exact time: 4:53 p.m. on February 5, 1883.

- When John is under Moriarty's thrall and repeating the words spoken into his earpiece, he says "Gottle o' geer" over and over. This is a joke amongst ventriloquists — you can spot an untrained ventriloquist when they try to make their dummy say "bottle of beer" without moving their lips. It comes out sounding like "gottle o' geer." By making John say it repeatedly, Moriarty is poking fun at John being his dummy.

- Sherlock, mocking the people who would hire Moriarty as their consulting criminal, says, "Dear Jim, will you please fix it for me to get rid of my lover's nasty sister?" He's alluding to the British television series *Jim'll Fix It*, starring British legend Jimmy Savile. He would read aloud letters from people who wrote in asking him to fix their problem, and then he would choose one (usually the letters from children) and fix it for them. The letters would begin, "Dear Jim, will you fix it for me to . . ." In a horrifying turn of events, this episode aired in 2010, Savile died in 2011, and in 2012 a sex scandal erupted where six decades of complaints against Savile came to light, and with the mountain of undeniable evidence, it was confirmed that Savile had sexually abused and raped people as young as five and as old as 75. Following the announcement, many monuments to Savile throughout Great Britain were removed, and the Savile family removed his grave's headstone and had it destroyed, expressing their deep regret about what had happened. All of his honors were revoked (honorary doctorates, streets named after him, statues). What has yet to be determined is how these complaints, going back decades, were somehow buried until after his death.

OOPS

- When Martin Freeman is standing in front of the fridge, watch how the skull on the table behind him disappears and reappears.
- When the news of Connie Prince's death first appears on the television, the news ticker reads "Make-over Queen Connie Prince dead at 48." But at the morgue, Lestrade points to the body and says, "Connie Prince, 54."
- Shooting at Semtex (C-4) would not actually detonate it; it requires a detonator or blasting cap. The sniper shot would have killed the elderly woman, but not exploded the bomb. Similarly, the end of this episode isn't much of a cliffhanger if you know that.

"I'm not a psychopath, Anderson. I'm a high-functioning sociopath. Do your research."

And with that one put-down in "A Study in Pink," Sherlock sparks one of the most heated debates in *Sherlock* fandom. Is Sherlock Holmes a psychopath or a sociopath? Or neither? What is the difference between the two? Is there a difference?

In the 19th century, doctors working with mental patients began noticing that some exhibited morally depraved behavior, and by the turn of the 20th century, those patients were referred to as "psychopaths." By the early 1940s, the term "sociopath" was being used to denote the damage that psychopathic behavior had on society, but it was generally used as a synonym for psychopathy. Today, many still argue that the two words describe exactly the same condition, while others maintain that the two conditions are quite distinct. To the latter group, a sociopath is someone whose psychopathic tendencies were caused by his or her environment and upbringing; a psychopath is someone who was born that way.

In 1980, the symptoms previously assigned to psychopathy were suddenly altered and then given a new name: antisocial personality disorder. The term "psychopathy" had focused on the personality of the individual; ASPD was defined by the individual's behavior in society. The shift caused enormous debate within the mental health community. Around the same time, criminal psychologist Dr. Robert Hare was working on what would ultimately become the Hare Psychopathy Checklist, a list of 20 items that could be used to indicate a high possibility that the patient exhibited psychopathic tendencies. The first half of the list refers to the patient's personality traits, whereas the second refers to the antisocial behaviors stemming from those personality traits, thus taking into consideration both sides of the coin.

According to Hare, "Most psychopaths . . . meet the criteria for ASPD, *but most individuals with ASPD are not psychopaths*" [emphasis his]. The complete list is as follows: "glibness and superficial charm, grandiose sense of self-worth, pathological lying, cunning/manipulative, lack of remorse, emotional shallowness, callousness and lack of empathy, unwillingness to accept responsibility for actions, a tendency to boredom, a parasitic lifestyle, a lack of realistic long-term goals, impulsivity, irresponsibility, lack of behavioral control, behavioral problems in early life, juvenile delinquency, criminal versatility, a history of 'revocation of conditional release' (i.e., broken parole), multiple marriages, and promiscuous sexual behavior." For each trait, the patient would score a 0 (no sign of that trait), 1 (shows some of that trait), or a 2 (fully exhibits that trait), and a score of at least 30 out of a possible 40 could lead to a diagnosis of psychopathy. Where a diagnosis of psychopathy seems to focus more on the personality traits of the person leaning to criminal behavior, a diagnosis of ASPD tends to derive from acting out the criminal behavior itself; far more people in prison have been diagnosed with ASPD than psychopathy (Hare estimates 50 to 75% of prisoners have ASPD, compared to 15 to 25% exhibiting traits of psychopathy).

So is Sherlock a sociopath? Sherlock certainly checks off many of the traits, especially when it comes to his lack of understanding of human emotions, but we also know that he is capable of attachments to others and deep emotion, as we see in the second and third seasons. He is deeply drawn to the criminal element, yet he uses his intellect to stop crime. Both Sherlock and Mycroft exhibit similar traits of coldness and isolation, which could point to a joint childhood trauma or genetics, yet they display their personalities in different ways. Experts have fallen resolutely on both sides of the argument, while others disagree with both assessments. Perhaps Sherlock is just irresponsible and childish, and needs to stop using his "I'm a sociopath!" declaration as an excuse, some say.

In the end, what matters in this scene isn't the diagnosis — it is, after all, a television program, and Sherlock exhibits traits of ASPD, psychopathy, schizoid personality disorder, schizophrenia, autism, and Asperger's, depending on the clinician you ask — but that Sherlock is able to put down Anderson so spectacularly in that moment that he leaves Anderson utterly speechless. Which is pretty much all Sherlock ever wants to do with his least favorite forensics expert.

SEASON TWO (2012)
Love, Fear, and Death

The first season of *Sherlock* introduced us to the central friendship; for season two of the show, Gatiss and Moffat decided to take on the three biggest foes Sherlock Holmes ever faced: the Woman, the Hound, and the Professor. It was a daring task — packing all of these legendary stories into a single short season rather than spreading them across several could have backfired — but it makes for a phenomenal sophomore outing.

Throughout the series, Sherlock insists that he's a high-functioning sociopath, even when his detractors prefer the phrase "psychopath" (see "Psychopath or Sociopath?" sidebar). The second season pits him against the heavy hitters of human emotions to see how he reacts. Irene Adler tests his ability to love, the Hound introduces fear and doubt into his usual robot-like way of seeing things, and Professor Moriarty returns to force Sherlock to face the greatest fear of all: death. But in each case, Sherlock experiences the emotion differently than others would. He doesn't fall in love so much as learn how people use love to gain an advantage; he doesn't fear the Hound, but instead fears the doubt that the possibility of the Hound instills within him; he doesn't react to Moriarty in the face of his own impending death so much as fear that the wrong action might cause the deaths of the people he cares about.

It's the way he deals with each of these emotions in season two that will largely change the way he interacts with the world around him in season three.

A SCANDAL IN BELGRAVIA

WRITTEN BY Steven Moffat
DIRECTED BY Paul McGuigan
ORIGINAL AIR DATE January 1, 2012

When Sherlock reluctantly agrees to take on a case, he is faced with one of the most legendary of his foes: the Woman, Irene Adler.

"Do you know the big problem with a disguise, Mr. Holmes? However hard you try, it's always a self-portrait," says Irene Adler, the only woman who ever beat Sherlock Holmes in the stories, who was more cunning than even Moriarty, and who is involved in the only case wherein Holmes asks to take away a sentimental keepsake: a photograph of her. In the finale to the first season, Sherlock says that the secret to disguise is hiding in plain sight. In this story, as in its literary counterpart, Sherlock must take on many disguises, but ultimately Adler sees through every one of them, eventually donning her own disguise that outdoes the best of his.

Moffat takes the idea of disguises and uses it as his key theme of this episode. No matter what mask each character wears, those who truly know them can see right through it. Sherlock pretends to be uncaring and aloof, but Mycroft knows that, above all else, Sherlock wants to impress. Mycroft acts as though a life of solitude is the only one for him, but whenever we see him alone, he looks unhappy, and the fact that he's constantly coming 'round to "two hundred and twenty-one bee" to see Sherlock suggests he doesn't value his alone time as much as he says he does. When Irene first enters the room to see Sherlock, she's entirely naked, but she wears her concern for her own well-being on her face, and Sherlock uses that vulnerability against her. And eventually, she reveals one card too many, which proves to be her undoing.

Whereas season one mapped out the beginning of the relationship between John and Sherlock, season two treats it like an established friendship with all of the advantages and problems that entails. The season two premiere opens exactly where the previous episode left off, with our heroes staring down their mortality in the face of Moriarty's game. In order to move into the new story at hand, the problem is done away with quickly, albeit hilariously, and, as John's blog title suggests, life goes on.

A lot of time passes in this first episode, and we see the seasons change and the friendship deepen between the two men. Now that John and Sherlock have had the poolside moment to deepen their bond, they are more at ease with one another. We see time pass as they work on cases, and rather than acting unsure of themselves as they move about the flat, they form an unbreakable team. John rolls his eyes at Sherlock's careless comments, while Sherlock peers over John's shoulder making caustic remarks about his blog entries. Their new, closer relationship offers a lot of opportunities for hilarity, especially in the alleyway when Sherlock asks John to punch him in the face. It's one of the highlights of the episode, but once again shows a strong friendship where they can punch each other in the face yet still remain pals afterwards. It's this ease and companionship that will become more important in the coming episodes.

One moment they're bickering via Skype as John tries to piece together a case on site while Sherlock is a complete jerk; the next they're sitting in Buckingham Palace, silent, unsure of how they got there. The scene of the two men on the couch is a wonderful moment because of the way it shows just how much their friendship has progressed. Until now we've only seen them share a laugh once, at the end of the first episode, when they knew something no one else did. But here all it takes is John asking Sherlock if he's wearing any pants — receiving a terse "No" in reply — for them to suddenly break down and giggle like schoolboys. The scene almost feels improvised, as if the actors couldn't keep straight faces after John's ridiculous question, and when John asks if they're here to see the queen, and Sherlock replies, "Apparently," just as Mycroft comes in, they lose all control.

Sherlock and John's relationship couldn't be more different from that of Sherlock and his brother. While it was clear in the previous season that Mycroft was a source of tension for Sherlock (and vice versa), this episode suggests the rift runs deep, all the way back to childhood. By setting Sherlock and John's friendship against this volatile sibling relationship, the bond between Sherlock and John is made that much stronger. One can assume that Mycroft has never jumped on a madman's back to save his little brother's life the way John did; similarly, Sherlock has not (yet) hurt John the way he hurts Mycroft at the end of this episode. Mycroft's entrance into the scene of two grown men acting like children is timed perfectly, for we immediately imagine that no such moment of hilarity has ever existed between the two Holmes boys. Mycroft prefers dignity and order, sits rigidly on the couch, announcing "I'll be Mother" as he pours the tea, and all shenanigans cease in his presence. There's no fondness apparent there, no inside jokes, and little respect for one another. Sherlock refuses to get dressed, and Mycroft berates him as he would a child.

Last season, we were shown the similarities between Mycroft and Sherlock, but in this episode the focus is on the differences.

Mycroft comes to Sherlock's flat and keeps his focus on the case, telling Mrs. Hudson to shut up when she interrupts him. Instead of continuing the conversation with Mycroft, both Sherlock and John, shocked that he could speak to their beloved landlady in such a way, shout at the elder Holmes and refuse to continue until he apologizes to her. Later in the episode, we see Sherlock in his flat on Christmas Eve surrounded by his friends — Watson and his latest girlfriend, Jeanette; Mrs. Hudson; Lestrade; and Molly Hooper — but when he calls Mycroft, his brother is sitting alone. Sherlock used to be like his brother, preferring a solitary existence to a social one, but John has helped push Sherlock into a different social sphere. As Sherlock becomes closer to John, he moves further away from his brother.

The key scene between the siblings is in the mortuary, when they go to identify Irene's body. Standing outside the room, Mycroft offers Sherlock a much-desired cigarette as a Christmas present, albeit a low-tar one ("you barely knew her"), and they stand beside one another, two outsiders looking at the world through a window, like spectators who are uninvolved in the lives outside. Mycroft looks at the people in the hospital corridor, obviously grieving over the very recent death of someone close to them. "Look at them," Sherlock says, "they all care so much. Do you ever think there's something wrong with us?" "Caring is not an advantage, Sherlock," Mycroft replies. In this gorgeously shot scene, Sherlock stands with Mycroft as if they are the same. But Mycroft sees through the guise and knows that Sherlock is no longer separate from the caring public, if he ever was. He knows that his brother cared about Irene Adler in some way, and that he simply exhibits his sorrow differently. As Sherlock leaves the mortuary, Mycroft calls John, and we discover that the two of them had been working behind Sherlock's back, united in their concern that the detective might fall victim to one of his many vices in his grief. It's an extraordinary moment: Sherlock and John have been positioned as being everything that Sherlock and Mycroft never were, with Mycroft on the outside looking in; yet here we see not only that John and Mycroft came together to help Sherlock, but that Mycroft's disguise of an uncaring person is disingenuous. He really *does* care about his little brother. He wants to be at home in front of a crackling fire on Christmas Eve, but instead he's standing in a mortuary, watching over his brother, and checking in with John to make sure he does the same thing. Both men care deeply for Sherlock, even if one of them has a tougher time showing it.

Sherlock's relationship with his brother is troubled, but his relationships with women are catastrophic (when there *is* any sort of relationship with a woman, which is rare). In the books, there is no end to Holmes's disparaging remarks about women or Watson's disgust at having to repeat them to his readers. In *The Sign of Four*, Holmes remarks, "Women are never to be entirely trusted — not the best of them." Watson editorializes, "I did not pause to argue over this atrocious statement."

What sets Adler's story apart from the others, however, is that the culprit isn't just a woman, but a woman who beats Sherlock at his own game. This is why, like Moriarty, the character appears in only one story but has appeared onstage and onscreen numerous times. The opportunity to show the complexity of gender relationships with Adler is immense, and therefore Moffat had a lot of pressure riding on his interpretation of this story. There has been a lot of criticism of the depiction of Irene Adler on *Sherlock* (the number of sites devoted to Moffat's inherent sexism as a writer are legion), but I have to disagree with it: not only is it a very faithful adaptation of the original character, but I do not think she was defeated in the way critics suggest she was.

This episode is based on "A Scandal in Bohemia," which is quite brief: Irene Adler is an opera singer and "adventuress" who was once the mistress of the King of Bohemia, who couldn't marry her because she was below his station and had a flawed moral character, in his eyes. He sent her love letters and a photograph of the two of them together, and now that he's about to marry a Scandinavian princess, he wants them back. Holmes, on the case, follows her to a church, where she's getting married, and she pulls Holmes in to witness the wedding.

Holmes returns to her house later that day disguised as a clergyman. She lets him in while Watson waits in the bushes outside the window; Holmes talks her into opening a window, Watson lets off a smoke bomb and yells, "Fire!" and Adler, in a panic, rushes to where the photograph is hidden. Watson and Holmes must leave because of the crowd that gathers. That evening, as Holmes is walking into his apartment, a boy walks by and says, "Good evening, Mr. Holmes." He looks up, thinking he knows the voice, but the youth is already gone. The next day Holmes returns to Adler's place with the King of Bohemia to get the materials from the hiding place Adler had inadvertently disclosed, but she has already left and taken everything with her. She leaves behind a photograph of herself and a letter telling Holmes she knew it was him in disguise, and that she was the youth who'd bid him good night. She says they will never find her, but she reassures the king that she has no intention of using the photo or letters; they are merely protection. Holmes requests as payment only her photograph, which he keeps with him for the rest of his life, always referring to her as *the* woman.

This story is played out rather faithfully in the first part of this episode. People have objected to Adler being a dominatrix in this 21st-century update, but "adventuress" was a negative term in the Victorian era, and an opera singer was seen as little more than a highly paid prostitute. Since both of these terms have a different meaning today, the writers had to convey Adler as a "fallen" woman for our times, which is difficult. So they made her like her Victorian counterpart: a strong woman who is proud of what she does, even if others might balk at it. She uses her job and position to get ahead in the world and make money, and refuses to be ruled by men. She leaves a sexy sigh on Sherlock's phone to indicate he has a text message, just as the Victorian Irene lets Holmes hear her voice one last time before she gets on a train. Doyle's Adler gets married and is forced out of London, on the run, left behind by a man who thought it inappropriate to marry her. *Sherlock*'s Irene practically brings down the British government, has Sherlock within her thrall, and is able to wrap him around her finger and use him for her own purposes. Not exactly a damsel in distress. And unlike the other Irene, not only is she *not* tied to the institution of marriage, she professes to be a lesbian.

The first time Sherlock sees Irene, she's completely naked, which has been deemed problematic by some viewers who saw her as being objectified onscreen in a way the male actors aren't. But we can't forget that Sherlock was starkers himself in the previous scene at Buckingham Palace. Adler does it to unnerve Sherlock, put him off his game, and make him unable to read her. Sherlock does it to piss off Mycroft, put him off *his* game, and get the upper hand. The only difference is Sherlock wraps himself in a sheet because he draws a line; Adler is shown as far more courageous and dominant, and has the nerve to walk in completely in the buff. Sherlock hides; she dares him to find what she's hiding. Immediately preceding this scene, we see the two of them performing the same operations: both flip through photos of the other one and think they know everything about that person; both go through several outfit choices, with her choosing nothing and him going with the same outfit he always wears, now with added clergyman collar. He figures out the combination to her safe — because she wants him to — and opens it, saving all of them, but, like her literary counterpart, Adler manages to get the information back and disappears.

Point: Adler.

This is the spot where the original story ends. But just like that seemingly unrelated case that Sherlock is working on, where the car backfires in the countryside and a man is found dead by a stream, Irene is the boomerang that turns around and whizzes back. It's no fun to have her just walk away (readers would expect that), so she chooses her second disguise: a dead body. She manages to interrupt the merriment of Christmas, fool Sherlock and Mycroft, discourage Molly, and send Sherlock into a spiral of despair. But not before she sends Sherlock her phone, putting him on a wild goose chase to come up with the passcode that will unlock it, a game that will consume Sherlock in the coming months.

Point: Adler.

For her next trick, she returns, and every time Sherlock thinks he's tricking her, she's already two steps ahead of him. Ultimately, she deceives him into undoing two years of British government plans, compromising himself, his brother, and all of Great Britain.

Point: Adler.

But wait! With Mycroft having no choice but to do her bidding, she shows one card too many — "Jim Moriarty sends his love" — and Sherlock solves her puzzle. For, despite the fact that Irene is a master of disguise and deceit, Sherlock knows Moriarty, the way he thinks and works, and it's through that slip that Sherlock gains the upper hand.

Point: Sherlock. (Sort of, given that it was a weakness in Moriarty's poker face — not Adler's — that gave it away. But she's the one who said Moriarty's name, so she loses this one.)

And now she's dead. Mycroft ensures that this death is real, and then forces John to lie to Sherlock for the first time. "It would take Sherlock to fool me," Mycroft tells John, "and I don't think he was on hand, do you?" But (cue music) Sherlock *was* on hand at her execution and prevented it. And therein lies the biggest problem some viewers have with this particular interpretation of Adler: in the end, she was a damsel to be saved by Sherlock. However, from a different perspective, it is *she* who had *him* in her thrall. When Sherlock thinks she is dead the first time, he doesn't mourn her out of love or attraction; he's sad that such a formidable foe is gone. When he instantly cracks her Bond Air code, it has nothing to do with the sexual favors she's promising him as she leans seductively over his desk, it's because he wants to impress someone as intelligent and cunning as her. He tells her that he took her pulse and knew that her heart was racing when she was around him, and that she was attracted to him, but that he remained distant. And yet, while Sherlock doesn't feel romantic love towards her, he is attracted to her mind and her brilliance the same way he always smiles at Moriarty with admiration, even when Moriarty is doing or saying terrible things to him. Notice when she drugs him, he doesn't have sexual fantasies about her, but instead fantasizes about her watching one of his deductions and being impressed by him. Her nakedness doesn't arouse him, it just throws him off his game. John, on the other hand, stammers, asks her to cover herself, and can't make eye contact. She doesn't slow down Sherlock's deductions by whispering untoward things in his ear, but once again she unnerves John. This woman who can use her own sexuality and cunning to overthrow governments and dominate people fascinates Sherlock. And for that, he will follow her to Karachi and save her life, because he doesn't want to lose such an impressive adversary. Knowing that Irene Adler is in the world makes it a little less dull for him, so now she has protection more powerful than anything on that phone.

Game: Adler.

Lara Pulver plays Adler with such fierceness and control, yet shows just the right hints of vulnerability and emotion that the audience can't help but side with her, even when Sherlock is showing her up.

Despite her bravura performance, however, one of the most memorable moments of this episode happens on Christmas Eve when Molly shows up in a stunning outfit, nervous and with a special present for Sherlock. The cocky detective is rarely kind to Molly (and even when he is, it's usually because he wants something from her), but the way he treats her in this scene is abhorrent. He not only embarrasses himself, but humiliates her in the process. Everyone in the room knows she's carrying a torch for Sherlock, but she believes she is hiding it behind her own mask. Everyone except Sherlock, however, immediately sees through the sexy "disguise" she wears to the party. The disdain he has for Molly stems not from a lack of attraction — Sherlock doesn't work that way — but from him believing she is not an intellectual equal, a girly-girl who just acts silly when she's around him. Her emotional reaction to his cruelty stops him in his tracks, and he suddenly realizes what he's done and what the true meaning behind her gift is, and he apologizes. It's a rare moment of humanity, one that's welcomed after such a terrible outburst, and yet another reason why fans love Molly so much. Louise Brealey is marvelous in this scene and, like Adler, is a woman who goes up against Sherlock in an argument and wins.

We have seen Sherlock's brotherly connection to John, admiration for Irene Adler, filial responsibility to Mycroft, and an apologetic kiss on Molly's cheek. But if there's one person that Sherlock actually does have feelings for, it's Mrs. Hudson. Sherlock isn't looking for any romantic attachments, but this mother figure is very important to him. He first admonishes Mycroft for being rude to her, as previously mentioned, but his true devotion to her unveils itself when he discovers she's in danger. When he enters 221, he knows before he even ascends the stairs that something terrible has happened to his landlady, and by the time he opens the door to 221B, he's ready. In most situations, Sherlock at first turns to reason and logic to gain the upper hand, but in this scene he moves straight to violence — and not just violence that will give him the advantage, but that exacts horrible and painful revenge over and over again. Like Irene and Molly, Mrs. Hudson shows that she's not a victim: she had exactly what the baddies were looking for hidden on her person the whole time. John worries that such a delicate woman should leave Baker Street to recover, but Sherlock knows how resilient Mrs. Hudson is. "Shame on you, John Watson," Sherlock says, to Mrs. Hudson's amusement. "Mrs. Hudson *leave* Baker Street? England would fall!"

"A Scandal in Belgravia" is a beautifully written and highly entertaining return to the second season, possibly the best script of the series to date. Mrs. Hudson holds her own, Molly gives Sherlock a stern talking-to, and Irene Adler breaks through Sherlock's resolute exterior and makes him care about her. It's a wonderful piece of subtle feminist storytelling, where every woman is strong and complex and manages to hold Sherlock in her thrall, even if just for a moment. After 18 months of waiting for a resolution to the big season-one cliffhanger, fans were treated to a return of all the series regulars, now with the stronger chemistry that a second season always promises. The script is often hilarious and yet also dives into the psychology of Sherlock's character with subtlety. It's wonderful to be back in 221B.

HIGHLIGHT The stunned look on John's face when Sherlock asks him to punch him in the face and then repeats the question when John doesn't answer. "Didn't you hear me?" "I *always* hear 'punch me in the face' when you're speaking," John replies, "but it's usually subtext."

DID YOU NOTICE?
- As Sherlock studies the body in the trunk of the car, he looks at the passport, which says the passenger's name is John Coniston. That's the name of the lead character on the BBC series *Inside Men*.
- When Irene whips Sherlock with a riding crop, it's similar to the way Sherlock was beating the dead body in "A Study in Pink."
- When Sherlock is reading the newspaper at the breakfast table, you can see the headline "Refit for Historical Hospital." For the big finale in the third episode of this season, the writers were originally going to involve some sort of scaffolding on St. Bart's, so they put the headline in the paper as a set-up. (The idea was later scrapped.)
- In the Christmas Eve scene — which ranks right up there with the drugs bust scene in "A Study in Pink" for pure entertainment — watch Lestrade in the background. The

look on his face when Molly removes her coat is price-less; when Sherlock tells him that his wife is having an affair, you can see him silently piecing it together and suddenly realizing it's true; and finally, when Sherlock's phone sighs with a new text and Molly says she didn't do that sound, Sherlock says, "No, it was me," and Lestrade immediately says, "Wait, *what*?!" Rupert Graves is spec-tacular.

- The woman who takes John to see Irene at the ware-house looks, dresses, and types on her phone the same way Anthea did in "A Study in Pink," and John clearly mistakes her for being the same woman, but it's a dif-ferent actress.

- At the end you can see all of Irene's texts:

  > I'm not hungry, let's have dinner.
  >
  > Bored in a hotel. Join me. Let's have dinner.
  >
  > John's blog is HILARIOUS. I think he likes you more than I do. Let's have dinner.
  >
  > I can see tower bridge and the moon from my room. Work out where I am and join me.
  >
  > I saw you in the street today. You didn't see me.
  >
  > You do know that hat actually suits you, don't you?
  >
  > Oh for God's sake. Let's have dinner.
  >
  > I like your funny hat.
  >
  > I'm in Egypt talking to an idiot. Get on a plane, let's have dinner.
  >
  > You looked sexy on Crimewatch.
  >
  > Even you have got to eat. Let's have dinner.
  >
  > BBC1 right now. You'll laugh.
  >
  > I'm thinking of sending you a Christmas present.
  >
  > Mantelpiece.
  >
  > I'm not dead. Let's have dinner.

FROM ACD TO BBC "A Scandal in Bohemia" is as much about disguises and masks as this episode is.

- In that story, Watson writes of Holmes that "the stage lost a fine actor, even as science lost an acute reasoner, when he became a specialist in crime."
- When the King of Bohemia arrives at Holmes's flat, he first tries to hide his identity from Holmes, but the sleuth sees through it instantly and forces him to remove his mask, just as a nearly naked Sherlock insists at Buckingham Palace that they reveal the name of his client.
- Holmes is disguised as a drunken groom when he gets hauled into Adler's wedding, and just as Sherlock dresses up as a priest who's been beaten up in the street, Holmes arrives at Adler's door dressed as a clergyman. He doesn't need Watson to punch him in the face because he stops a purse-snatching in the street and gets roughed-up in the process (though he does add fake blood).

Several of Doyle's story titles are played with in this episode: "The Greek Interpreter" becomes "The Geek Interpreter"; "The Adventure of the Speckled Band" becomes "The Speckled Blonde"; a case Sherlock scathingly refers to as the Belly Button Murders is titled "The Navel Treatment" by John, a riff on "The Naval Treaty."

When Sherlock is called out to investigate a body in the trunk of a car, he says he has eight ideas, which he narrows to four, and then two. In several of the stories, Holmes says he has a specific number of theories upon looking at the scene, such as in "The Adventure of the Copper Beeches" when he says he has "seven separate explanations."

In *The Sign of Four* and "The Boscombe Valley Mystery,"

Holmes says he can differentiate between 140 types of tobacco ash; on the show, the number is inflated to 243.

Mrs. Hudson opens the refrigerator and finds a bag of thumbs. In "The Adventure of the Engineer's Thumb," a client rushes into 221B with his hand still bleeding from where his thumb had just been lopped off.

In "The Adventure of the Illustrious Client," Holmes refuses to take on a case if they won't reveal the identity of the client to him, no matter how urgent the case may be. In this episode, Sherlock is just as stubborn, and when he outright asks who the client is, the equerry simply replies, "Illustrious."

The equerry at Buckingham Palace says to John that his employer is a big fan of John's blog and "particularly enjoyed the one about the aluminium crutch." In "The Musgrave Ritual," Watson and Holmes discuss the cases that Watson has written about, and Holmes says they weren't all winners, mentioning "the singular affair of the aluminum crutch." Since this is a story never explained in the canon, fans can only imagine what the case could have been. It will be mentioned again in the next episode.

John mentions that the counter on his blog has been stuck at 1895 for some time. At the beginning of "The Adventure of Black Peter," Watson writes, "I have never known my friend to be in better form, both mental and physical, than in the year '95." Many of the stories are set in this year.

Just before opening Adler's safe, Sherlock yells "Vatican cameos!" and John ducks. Despite the nonsense on the internet that it's a phrase originating in World War II that was a British code for "duck," it's actually a reference to the beginning of Doyle's *The Hound of the Baskervilles*, where Holmes explains he had gotten very involved in a case he was working for the Pope wherein he was searching for Vatican cameos. John and

Sherlock have clearly come up with a series of code words in certain dangerous situations, and this is one of them. (It will be used again in the third season.)

Irene Adler beats Sherlock with a riding crop; in "The Adventure of the Six Napoleons," Watson comments that Holmes brings along a "loaded hunting-crop, which was his favourite weapon."

On the wall of Sherlock's bedroom is a periodic table and the rules of bartitsu, a form of martial arts popular at the turn of the 19th century in England. In "The Adventure of the Empty House," Sherlock reveals that he was able to beat Moriarty using "baritsu" [*sic*] and referred to it as a Japanese style of wrestling.

In "The Adventure of the Dying Detective," Watson notes that Holmes "had a remarkable gentleness and courtesy in his dealings with women. He disliked and distrusted the sex, but he was always a chivalrous opponent."

INTERESTING FACTS

- The title of this episode, like all *Sherlock* titles that are plays on Doyle story titles, alters "Bohemia" to "Belgravia." Belgravia is a very upscale area in London, presumably where Irene's flat is located (though that's never stated outright). However, *Belgravia* was also the name of a 19th-century literary magazine within which Sir Arthur Conan Doyle had some of his earliest stories published (though none featuring Sherlock Holmes).
- Producer Sue Vertue has said that the idea for the "Stayin' Alive" ringtone on Moriarty's phone came from an actual incident where she was at a funeral and someone's phone began ringing with that same ringtone at a very inappropriate moment. The irony was both horrifying and hilarious.

- Sherlock grabs the deerstalker hat as a disguise, but is photographed in the hat and it immediately becomes his trademark, even though that's not his intention. The moment is a clever nod to the fact that Sir Arthur Conan Doyle never actually mentioned Sherlock wearing a deerstalker, but illustrator Sidney Paget drew him wearing one. Just as John will later refer to the deerstalker as a "Sherlock hat," it's now immediately identifiable as belonging to Sherlock Holmes.

- John's girlfriend Jeanette is played by Oona Chaplin, daughter of Geraldine Chaplin, granddaughter of Charlie Chaplin, and great-granddaughter of Eugene O'Neill. She is perhaps best known to North American audiences as Talisa Maegyr on *Game of Thrones*.

- John referring to his middle name as "Hamish" is an inside joke among longtime Sherlockians. Sir Arthur Conan Doyle was notoriously inconsistent in the stories, and in one story — "The Man with the Twisted Lip" — Watson's wife, Mary, refers to him as "James." To try to compensate for Doyle's inaccuracy and instead come up with a proper explanation, detective fiction author Dorothy L. Sayers wrote an article suggesting that perhaps his middle initial — "H," which is never expanded — stands for Hamish, which is the Scottish form of James, and Mary was referring to him by that middle name as a pet name. Unlikely, but Moffat gives it a nod in this episode.

- Adler says she has a safety deposit box in the Strand, which is a reference not only to the place but to *Strand* magazine, which published most of the Holmes stories.

- Mycroft uses the word "Coventry" when talking about the Bond Air operation, and Sherlock connects it to an incident — which he says is "probably not true" — where Winston Churchill knew that Coventry was going to be bombed because his code breakers at Bletchley Park had decoded the German mission, but rather than give up the fact that he was decoding their messages, he let Coventry burn. It's a story that has been passed down for decades, but Churchill insiders insist it's not true. According to most sources on the inside, they knew the Germans were going to be bombing part of England in a mission that was code-named "Moonlight Sonata," but they had no idea where the bombs were going to be dropped. On the evening of November 14, 1940, Churchill was on his way home, reading through that day's notes, and he became convinced London was going to be the target. He turned the car around and headed back into London, determined to be present if his city was going to burn that night. He sat all night in an air-raid shelter, occasionally going to the rooftops to look for action, but nothing happened. They had no idea that miles away, Coventry was being bombed, and they had just never gotten the proper information. Conspiracy theorists, however, don't believe this story and maintain that Churchill sacrificed the West Midland town for the greater good.

NITPICKS

- Despite the fact that Irene enters the room naked, couldn't Sherlock have deduced *something* about her — beyond her body measurements? A lot could be said about her hair, her makeup, her blood-red lipstick, her perfectly manicured nails, her stare, the room and its contents . . . even the fact that she's chosen nudity to throw him off his game.

- How is it that Sherlock can look at a string of numbers and decipher it in under five seconds, but it takes him an eternity to connect "double-oh seven" to James Bond? Perhaps he needs to declutter that mind palace?

OOPS The sign over the mortuary door says "Morgue," but in St. Bart's the room is actually the mortuary, like in all British hospitals.

THE HOUNDS
OF BASKERVILLE

WRITTEN BY Mark Gatiss

DIRECTED BY Paul McGuigan

ORIGINAL AIR DATE January 8, 2012

Sherlock and John travel to the moors to investigate a sighting of a gigantic hound.

Doyle's third Sherlock Holmes novel, *The Hound of the Baskervilles*, is his most enduring, and the Doyle story that has had more adaptations than any other. A man, Dr. Mortimer, comes to Baker Street and reports that the current resident of the great Baskerville estate reportedly died of a heart attack, but Mortimer believes he was murdered. He explains the family curse — the Baskervilles have been haunted by a giant hellhound since the 18th century, and that when he investigated the area where Baskerville had died, he saw something — and utters the now-legendary line, "Mr. Holmes, they were the footprints of a gigantic hound!" The heir to the Baskerville fortune, Sir Henry Baskerville, is coming over from Canada, and Mortimer is worried he will suffer the same fate. Holmes sends Watson to investigate, saying he is unable to come. At the estate, Watson discovers that someone has been stealing Sir Henry's boots. Watson meets Mr. Stapleton, the local naturalist, who tells him about the great Grimpen Mire, a vast bog that regularly swallows up dogs, horses, and people, since no one but he knows where to step. Stapleton's sister tries to warn Watson away. Watson discovers there is a murderer loose on the moors and that the Baskerville butler, Barrymore, is related to the murderer by marriage and has been signaling warnings to him using a candle in a window. Barrymore shows Watson a partially burned letter that he suspects was sent to Baskerville the night he died, sent by the daughter of local curmudgeon Mr. Frankland.

Watson sends regular reports back to London, which make up most of the narrative in the novel. One night, old man Frankland tells Watson that he believes the killer is on the moor, because he's seen a young man carrying out food to someone. Watson investigates and finds none other than Holmes, who has been holed up in a cave all this time, receiving Watson's reports and doing his own investigation, always a few steps ahead. In the climax of the novel, Holmes and Watson discover the motive in the case, and as a fog rolls in, they travel out onto the moor where they do, indeed, encounter the hound — covered in phosphorous by the perpetrator to make it glow in the dark. At the sound of the hound's howl, Holmes is legitimately unnerved: "'Where is it?' Holmes whispered; and I knew from the thrill of his voice that he, the man of iron, was shaken to the soul." Later, as they spot the hound and try to get away, Watson says of Holmes's escape, "Never have I seen a man run as Holmes ran that night." As they pursue the culprit behind the entire escapade, the offender gets caught in the Grimpen Mire and is sucked down to his death.

As an adaption of an original story, Gatiss's script is stunning. Knowing that audiences have seen it all before — the hound, the mire, Sir Henry's boots, the suspects, Holmes and Watson being separated — and that everyone who has read the book or seen one of its many adaptations would know the ending, he upends it and, using all of Doyle's elements, rearranges many of them, modernizes the story, and changes the eventual outcome. When it comes to adapting Doyle's material, Gatiss is the master. The phosphorous hound becomes a glowing bunny named Bluebell.

The Stapletons — the naturalist and his "sister" — become the scientist with questionable ethics and her daughter, who similarly is a "Miss Stapleton" who sounds the alarm for Sherlock. Sir Henry Baskerville becomes the cleverly named Henry Knight, who is not the heir to the Baskerville fortune, for "Baskerville" has gone from being a family name to the name of a large genetic testing facility. The Grimpen Mire becomes the Grimpen Minefield (with similar results); cranky old Frankland becomes the friendly (or *is* he?) Dr. Frankland; Barrymore the butler becomes Major Barrymore; and Dr. Mortimer, the man concerned for the welfare of the Baskerville family, becomes Louise Mortimer, Henry's therapist.

Even if you know the original story, Gatiss keeps you guessing; he delights the knowledgeable Sherlockian while entertaining.

However, as a script that can stand on its own, it's not as successful. For those who aren't familiar with the original story, all of the red herrings don't make a lot of sense. Why are we sent on a wild goose chase for the origins of Bluebell when it doesn't seem to have anything to do with the rest of the story? What are the chances that Sherlock, out of boredom, takes the only case that remotely interests him and it just *happens* to coincide with the more interesting case that walks through his door? Why would Sherlock take on a case that, on its surface, doesn't actually interest him, merely because of the old-fashioned way the client refers to the dog? As the catalyst for Sherlock's actions, it seems silly. Why does the UMQRA red herring go on for so long? It's a hilarious payoff for the reader — the woman in the car sensually moans, "Oh, Mr. Selden!" which is the name of the murderer signaling to Baskerville Hall from the moor — but without knowing that, it just seems like a really long diversion that keeps John out of the way.

Where the episode succeeds for all audiences is when it becomes a study in fear. When Henry Knight first appears, he's quiet, fidgety, tired-looking, and on the verge of tears. It's brilliant casting; Russell Tovey, at the time, was starring on BBC's *Being Human* as George, the flatmate who happens to turn into a werewolf every full moon. On that show, he plays a charming man who is deathly afraid of the agony of his monthly transformation. In this episode, the dynamic is flipped, and he plays the one afraid of the beast. Tovey is amazing as he fears being forced back out onto the moors; as he awakes from yet another nightmare; as he stands at his patio window and sees a hound's face smash into it (in the scariest moment of the series); and as he realizes with horror that he almost killed another human being in a hallucinogenic haze.

Knight brings not only the case to Sherlock, but the dread that accompanies it. Until now, Sherlock has very rarely shown fear of any kind. Even as he was about to put the pill in his mouth in "A Study in Pink," he looked mostly confident in his decision. As he mounted the stairs in "A Scandal in Belgravia," knowing he would find the criminals who had hurt Mrs. Hudson, he walked with vengeful purpose. In "The Blind Banker," when Sarah was staring at an arrow that was about to whiz toward her head and Sherlock had a gun pointed at his, he kept his hands in his pockets and coolly talked to General Shan. As a child in the line of fire counted down from 10 and Sherlock had to act quickly in "The Great Game," he looked anxious but not scared. Even when John stepped out onto the pool deck and was covered in explosives, the look on Sherlock's face had far more surprise in it than fear.

But in this episode, Sherlock is truly scared. Just as the love he feels for Irene Adler isn't a traditional sort of romantic love, the terror he feels in this episode isn't for his own safety; it's the fear of not knowing what is real. If the hound does indeed exist, then everything he ever believed to be true and untrue is suddenly called into question. What he saw couldn't be explained away by logic or science, and Sherlock is unable to function in such a world. At the Cross Keys pub, he is frantic, shaking, and angry, filled with uncertainty and acting in a way we haven't seen before. Contrast his behavior in this scene to the beginning of the episode when he's bored: he's also frantic, rude, and angry as he searches for his cigarettes, but in a different way that we already associate with Sherlock. Bored Sherlock causes John to roll his eyes in frustration; doubtful Sherlock causes John to leave the pub in anger. Cumberbatch does an extraordinary job of creating a very subtle, yet meaningful, difference between the two emotions.

But of the three performances, the one given by Martin Freeman is the standout. When Sherlock doesn't understand something, he experiments on it until he does. In *A Study in Scarlet*, when Mike Stamford first tells Watson about Holmes (with a note of warning in his voice), he says, "I could imagine his giving a friend a little pinch of the latest vegetable alkaloid, not out of malevolence, you understand, but simply out of a spirit of inquiry in order to have an accurate idea of the effects. To do him justice, I think that he would take it himself with the same readiness." In this episode, he does exactly that. Under the guise of the apologetic friend who wants to make it up to John for acting like a jerk in the pub the previous evening, Sherlock makes John a coffee, stirring in the very sugar he'd imbibed the day before, *convinced* it contains a hallucinogenic agent that caused him and Henry to see the hound when John didn't. He then stages an elaborate psychological test that nearly scares the life out of John, enhancing his own experience with bright lights and screeching sounds. The sadistic experiment frightens John to such an extent that he ends up cowering inside a cage, so terrified he can barely speak into his mobile phone when he calls Sherlock in a panic. Freeman is astounding in this scene: at first confused, then increasingly scared, and finally so filled with terror you swear you can see the hairs on his head turning gray before your eyes. When he emerges from the cage, he's gasping for air, barely able to stand up, screaming at Sherlock that the hound was there, and he's convinced of it. Of all the suspenseful moments in this episode, Freeman's performance makes this scene the most memorable.

Ultimately, the entire thing comes down to psychology and science, and the planets in Sherlock's world happily realign (even if, due to his lack of interest in the solar system, he's unaware of it). The solution to the case works both as an adaptation and simply on its own, as Gatiss continues to jar our expectations yet remains faithful to the sensibility of the story. John discovers what Sherlock tried to do to him, but he remains satisfied that Sherlock was wrong, and that he can throw that in his face as often as he likes in retaliation. Their friendship is intact, and unlike the Holmes of the novel, who deceives Watson and upsets him without a proper apology, this Sherlock stands by John's side . . . even if it's just to experiment on him.

However, Gatiss isn't going to let the warm feeling of a satisfactory ending sit with us for long. The episode ends jarringly, with Mycroft standing in a room with Moriarty, telling him he's free to go. Covering the walls is Sherlock's name written over and over again; in case we've forgotten who Sherlock saw flash before his eyes during his hallucination of the hound, we're reminded in this eerie scene. We've seen Sherlock deal with love and fear. We know what comes next.

HIGHLIGHT John explaining to Sherlock that they will never play Cluedo (or Clue) again.

Sherlock: Why not?

John: Because it's not actually possible for the victim to have done it, Sherlock, that's why.

Sherlock: Well, it was the only possible solution.

John: It's not in the rules.

Sherlock: Then the rules are wrong!

DID YOU NOTICE?

- John not only makes a crack about Sherlock having Asperger's when he's talking to Lestrade, but calls Sherlock "Spock" when Sherlock's coming undone in the pub. Interestingly, John calls him that right after Sherlock's famed line from the books, "Once you've ruled out the impossible, whatever remains — however improbable — must be true." In the film *Star Trek VI: The Undiscovered Country*, Spock utters the same line and attributes it to an "ancestor" of his.

- "Watson's Theme" begins playing when John is scared in the lab, and the music becomes increasingly discordant as his terror grows.

FROM ACD TO BBC Aside from the major points in *The Hound of the Baskervilles*, as pointed out earlier, Gatiss alludes to the novel in subtler ways:

- At first Sherlock says John will have to go alone, then says he's just kidding, that of course he's coming along, a reference to the fact that Holmes is missing for most of the novel.

- At the beginning of the story, Holmes asks Watson to try a deduction, and when Watson misses all of the key points but still comes up with some good observations, Holmes mocks him: "It may be that you are not yourself luminous, but you are a conductor of light. Some people without possessing genius have a remarkable power of stimulating it." Sherlock uses those words in his apology to John.

- Just as John is hurt by Sherlock's rudeness at the pub, Watson is deeply hurt when he discovers that Holmes has been deceiving him by investigating the case as well. He recounts that moment: "'You use me, and yet do not trust me!' I cried with some bitterness. 'I think that I have deserved better at your hands, Holmes.'" Later he says, "My voice trembled as I recalled the pains and the pride with which I had composed [my reports]." And just as Sherlock apologizes to John the following day and all is well, Holmes tells Watson that his reports had actually been quite helpful and shows the worn papers to him. Watson says he forgives Holmes because of the warmth in the detective's voice.

At the very beginning of the episode, Sherlock appears in the apartment holding a harpoon and covered in blood. In "The Adventure of Black Peter," Watson says that one morning Holmes "had gone out before breakfast, and I had sat down to mine when he strode into the room, his hat upon his head and a huge barbed-headed spear tucked like an umbrella under his arm." He had apparently been stabbing a dead pig at the butcher's to see how much strength is required to kill one.

In his frustration, Sherlock says to John that he envies him: "Your mind, it's so placid, straightforward, barely used. Mine's like an engine, racing out of control; a rocket tearing itself to pieces trapped on the launch pad." In "The Adventure of Wisteria Lodge," Holmes similarly describes his brain: "My mind is like a racing engine, tearing itself to pieces because it is not connected up with the work for which it was built."

Fletcher is the kid who wears the hound mask and scares tourists. His name is probably an homage to Bertram Fletcher Robinson, to whom Doyle dedicated the novel for giving him the idea of the story.

Sherlock gets information from Fletcher by telling him a bet is riding on it. In "The Adventure of the Blue Carbuncle," Holmes is able to extract information out of someone simply by betting the person that he can't. As he later explains to Watson, "I daresay that if I had put £100 down in front of him, that man would not have given me such complete information as was drawn from him by the idea that he was doing me on a wager."

We discover in this episode that Lestrade's name is Greg. In "The Adventure of the Cardboard Box," Lestrade signs one of his telegrams "G. Lestrade," and the first initial is never explained. A running joke in upcoming episodes will be Sherlock calling Lestrade by every other name that begins with G, but never Greg, which is a nod to all of the various names that Sherlockians have suggested the G stands for over the years. Perhaps the writers went with Greg because, in the books, Holmes primarily deals with two detectives, Lestrade and Gregson.

Sherlock observes that Lestrade is "as brown as a nut." When Stamford first meets Watson upon Watson's return from Afghanistan, Stamford notes, "You are as thin as a lath and as brown as a nut."

Sherlock's famous line to John at the Cross Keys is reworded from the original that appears in *The Sign of Four*: "How often have I said to you that when you have eliminated the impossible, whatever remains, *however improbable*, must be the truth?" He repeats the line in several other stories, including "The

Adventure of the Blanched Soldier" and "The Adventure of the Bruce-Partington Plans."

Sherlock's assertion that he has no friends upsets John, and later, during Sherlock's hamfisted apology, he explains that what he meant was that he only has one friend, not friends plural. In "The Five Orange Pips," when Watson mentions Holmes's "friends," Holmes corrects him: "Except yourself I have none."

One of the things that tips off Sherlock to Frankland's guilt is that he refers to a cellphone, rather than a mobile phone, indicating he'd spent time in the U.S. In "The Adventure of the Three Garridebs," Holmes similarly sniffs out a criminal for using the American spelling of a word (plow) rather than the British (plough).

The twist at the end of this episode is that the Hound is an apparition caused by inhaling hallucinogenic gas. In "The Adventure of the Devil's Foot," after a series of occurrences where people are found dead, still sitting upright as if alive, Holmes discovers that hallucinogenic gas is being pumped into the rooms. He and Watson attempt to test it, and Watson describes the feeling of beginning to go mad, as Holmes simply sits in his chair with a look of horror on his face. Watson grabs Holmes and pulls him out of the room to save both their lives.

INTERESTING FACTS

- Sherlock and John's argument about Cluedo (or Clue, as it's called in North America) is a clever wink at the game's origins. When Hasbro released the game in 1949, they marketed it as "The Great New Detective Game," with a picture on the front of the box of a detective in a long plaid cape and deerstalker looking through a magnifying glass. Hasbro then made a licensing deal with the Sir Arthur Conan Doyle estate to use the name "Sherlock Holmes" in their marketing materials, announcing to consumers that this game would allow them to become the great detective himself. In the 1970s, a TV commercial for the game featured Watson and Holmes trying to seek out clues.

- When Sherlock is sitting in the pub, shaken after seeing the hound, he says to Watson, *"Cherchez le chien."* It's a clever turn on the sexist phrase *"cherchez la femme"*: if a man is acting strangely, look for the woman, because his behavior must be the responsibility of a woman.

- Dr. Stapleton tells John that the rabbits glowed because of GFP, or green fluorescent protein, thanks to the presence of the gene from jellyfish that makes them glow. In 2008, the Nobel Prize in Chemistry was awarded to scientists who isolated and extracted the gene, while other researchers have successfully inserted GFP into developing embryos of zebrafish, causing them to glow.

NITPICKS Let me get this straight: there's a top-secret government project that is so classified only the highest CIA official would be given clearance, but they have their own *sweatshirts* with not only the name of the secret project emblazoned on the front of them, but the location of where the project was being carried out? And then when Frankland was using the top-secret hallucinogenic to kill Henry's father that night, he just happened to be wearing the sweatshirt? Were they testing the hallucinogenics on themselves?!

OOPS

- In the British army, one does not salute an officer who is not in uniform; one instead stands at attention. But when John reveals that he is, in fact, an officer, the soldier instantly salutes him.

- Watch the top of your screen closely when John climbs out of the cage in a frenzy, pacing back and forth as he talks to Sherlock. At one point, the camera cranes too high and you can see the studio lights and edge of the set.
- When Sherlock is trying to discover Barrymore's password, he finds a photograph of a young Barrymore with his father and says he has a Distinguished Service Order ribbon that places him in the 1980s. However, Barrymore is not wearing the 1980s DSO but the Conspicuous Gallantry Cross, which replaced the DSO and wasn't issued until 1995.

THE MIND PALACE

In "The Hounds of Baskerville," Sherlock's thought process is referred to as his "mind palace" for the first time in the series. In *A Study in Scarlet*, Holmes gives a detailed explanation of how his mind works, and it has been quoted in part by nearly every incarnation of the character since:

> *I consider that a man's brain originally is like a little empty attic, and you have to stock it with such furniture as you choose. A fool takes in all the lumber of every sort that he comes across, so that the knowledge which might be useful to him gets crowded out, or at best is jumbled up with a lot of other things, so that he has a difficulty in laying his hands upon it. Now the skilful workman is very careful indeed as to what he takes into his brain-attic. He will have nothing but the tools which may help him in doing*

his work, but of these he has a large assortment, and all
in the most perfect order. It is a mistake to think that that
little room has elastic walls and can distend to any extent.
Depend upon it there comes a time when for every addition
of knowledge you forget something that you knew before. It
is of the highest importance, therefore, not to have useless
facts elbowing out the useful ones.

Holmes's explanation is in response to Watson, soon after meeting him, inexplicably drawing up a list of everything the great detective *doesn't* know, including astronomy. Later, in "The Five Orange Pips," Holmes brings up the idea again and explains, "A man should keep his little brain-attic stocked with all the furniture that he is likely to use, and the rest he can put away in the lumber-room of his library, where he can get it if he wants it."

Leave it to Benedict Cumberbatch's Sherlock to convert Holmes's "brain-attic" into a palace. In season one, the mind palace is pictured as a series of words and phrases that appear onscreen (as when Sherlock is investigating the corpse of the woman dressed in pink), or a series of maps and road signs (as when he and John are chasing the taxicab through the streets of London). In "The Hounds of Baskerville," we actually watch from the outside as Sherlock enters his mind palace, and we see the stream-of-consciousness of his brain patterns moving from one item to the next. His eyes are closed, and his hands flick away the unnecessary words and images while reorganizing in the air the ones he needs. And when he finally hits upon the answer, his entire body jolts, as if he didn't see the solution coming. In season three, the writers take it one step further: rather than keep the audience on the outside, we're invited inside the mind palace and see its corridors, rooms, and doorways, and the prominent items — and people — that reside there.

Sherlock's mnemonic patterns are a method of loci, a system of building up a mind palace or memory palace that goes back to ancient Greece and Rome. The idea is simple — imagine a series of rooms, and commit certain items to those rooms. As one walks through the memory palace of one's mind, one can remember every item stored in there simply by looking at the various shelves and drawers where the items have been stored. Participants in memory competitions use the technique; they are asked to remember a series of numbers or playing cards, and then to repeat them back in the same order. By pre-assigning a mental image to each card or number and a place in the memory palace, the best competitors are able to do it quickly and easily. The technique is used and taught by British mentalist Derren Brown, who is a longtime friend of Mark Gatiss and appears in *Sherlock*'s third season.

THE REICHENBACH FALL

WRITTEN BY Stephen Thompson

DIRECTED BY Toby Haynes

ORIGINAL AIR DATE January 15, 2012

Jim Moriarty returns to make everyone question everything they ever thought they knew about Sherlock.

"Oh, I may be on the side of the angels, but don't think for *one second* that I am one of them."

We've giggled at Sherlock's arrogance, laughed out loud at his putdowns directed at the police force, and shaken our heads when he mocks John for being a less intelligent life form than him. But in "The Reichenbach Fall," Sherlock's hubris turns out to be his (almost) fatal flaw.

When people first meet Sherlock, they can't help but be impressed. When he looks at John's phone and deduces John's situation, his personal wealth, and family secrets, we're all amazed. John is in awe, and Sherlock basks in the pride of knowing he just mesmerized his new friend. But very quickly it starts to get tired. Some of Doyle's stories begin with Holmes staring at Watson and saying something that would suggest he's reading his mind. By the time he explains that Watson looked up from his paper, checked his watch, looked out the window, stared at a painting, looked back at the paper, and then glanced at the bookshelf and *therefore* must have been thinking of the Afghan war, every reader's patience is growing a little thin. Similarly, we see John trying to get Sherlock to stop "showing off" all the time. In "The Blind Banker," Sebastian mocks Sherlock and says people hated him for doing his thing. In "The Hounds of Baskerville," Sherlock begins deducing things about Henry's train trip and John tells him he's showing off, to which Sherlock (suffering through nicotine withdrawal) bellows, "Of course, I *am* a show-off. That's what we do." Henry, on the other hand, is wonderstruck by Sherlock's genius.

Moriarty loved watching Sherlock in action in the first season. Moriarty's closest interaction with Sherlock was through Jeff the cab driver in "A Study in Pink," but in "The Great Game," Moriarty speaks indirectly to Sherlock by forcing others to repeat his words, like some deranged Cyrano de Bergerac. He tells Sherlock — through one of his bomb-laden victims — that he loves to watch him dance. He puts Sherlock through one test after another, delighting at seeing the great detective at work. When he meets Sherlock at the pool, he seems to enjoy every moment, and even tells Sherlock he can't bring himself to kill him (he's saving that for another day). Moriarty can't stand the thought of being the only person on the planet so ingenious, so when it's Sherlock's time to die, Moriarty wants to make it special.

In "A Scandal in Belgravia," Sherlock revealed to Adler that he had taken her pulse, and that was how he knew what she was thinking when she was coming on to him. But when she agreed to help Moriarty decode a message by going through Sherlock, she was allowing Moriarty to take Sherlock's pulse, to size up the situation and see if he would fall for her tricks. What Sherlock does for Irene is show off. As Mycroft later said, Sherlock is so caught up in trying to impress Adler that he doesn't pause to consider what information he might be giving to her. Realizing that with a little bit of praise, Sherlock's pride would be so strong he'd lose sight of his morality, Moriarty uses that hubris against him.

As Sherlock's fame grows and he becomes more recognizable — to John's chagrin, since a private detective's very occupa-
tion relies on anonymity — he becomes more aloof and distant,
tossing aside meaningful gifts from people and making snide
remarks about their usefulness. John has to play the good cop to
Sherlock's bad one more and more, and when Sherlock encounters Kitty in the men's washroom, he doesn't have John nearby to
soften what he says. He's vicious in his deduction of who she is,
becoming more menacing as he leans in and says, "You . . . repel
. . . me." By the time he gets to Moriarty's trial, all Sherlock does
is scoff at the jury and the judge and show off, even correcting
the barrister questioning him, much to Moriarty's delight. The
villain stands in the dock, chomping on gum and smirking as he
watches the room become more uncomfortable in Sherlock's
presence than in his own, until Sherlock, unsurprisingly, goes
one step too far and ends up in the cell beside Moriarty. There's
a wonderful cinematic moment when Sherlock's back is to us as
he enters the cell, and Moriarty is on the other side of the wall,
facing us. Sherlock turns to look forward, and Moriarty turns his
back on us. Yin and yang indeed.

Sherlock wants the world to see how smart he is — a vulnerability Moriarty is only too happy to exploit. It's why he
sent Adler to get Sherlock to decode the seat numbers on the
Bond Air jet, because he knew Sherlock would want to impress
her. Sherlock's face is all over the papers, whereas Moriarty
traditionally works anonymously, using conduits to act as his
mouthpieces. When Moriarty pulls off the perfect criminal
trifecta at the beginning of the episode, breaking into the
Tower of London (Andrew Scott is marvelous in this scene as
he dances his way up to the glass case), the Bank of England,
and Pentonville Prison simultaneously, he risks having a
more recognizable face than Sherlock's. But even with these

high-profile stunts, he redirects attention back to the detective, first by writing "GET SHERLOCK" in giant letters on the glass, then by having his lawyer call him to the witness stand in his trial. At this point he's got all of the puzzle pieces together to reveal the end of his long con: pinning everything on Sherlock. Moriarty knew cops like Anderson and Donovan suspected Sherlock anyway; he knew when he let him go at the pool that Sherlock's hubris would put his face in all the papers; he knew that everyone perceives the sleuth's deductions to be almost like magic tricks. So it was time to reveal the biggest trick of all: that Sherlock was Moriarty all along.

The scene where Jim reveals that he is actually Richard Brook, a small-time actor who has been used and abused by Sherlock, is superb. Jim cowers in the corner, holding his arms in front of him, his hair messy, his shirt unclean, looking like a man who is exhausted by having to play the villain when really he's just "The Storyteller." At first the viewer scoffs at Kitty's gullibility and the nerve Moriarty has to think he can so easily do away with Sherlock. But then Kitty pulls out Richard Brook's CV, press clippings, interviews, and "Richard" begs them to look at the DVD as his voice wavers in fear before the dark specter of Sherlock. The real magic of this scene is looking at the faces of everyone in it. Kitty is smug, because she is thrilled to know that the man so repelled by her is actually a master villain. John just looks confused, never wavering in his belief in Sherlock. Jim looks terrified, with his back against the wall and his eyes wide with horror. As Kitty rushes over to the corner to get the CV and John is talking to her, Jim rubs his hands over his face, then pulls his hands aside and looks at Sherlock, a goofy smile spreading over his face as if to say, "Gotcha!" And Sherlock's reaction is the best of all. He stands as if in awe, the reality of what Moriarty has done dawning on him, a "why didn't *I* think of that first" look on his face. He stares at Jim, mouth slightly open, as Jim grins at him, and a smile twitches in the corner of Sherlock's mouth.

He is impressed. *Really* impressed.

But the awe quickly passes, and the fury sets in. He growls at Moriarty and yells at him the way a parent would a child to *"Stop it NOW!"* before he chases him up the stairs. It's a fantastic scene, capped by Kitty's haughty "You repel me" line hissed at Sherlock as he runs out the door.

Since Moriarty works alone, there's no one who could refute his charges (except for Sherlock). Tell the world that you're a nobody, and all eyes are suddenly upon the detective and off you. We live in a society that takes great pleasure in seeing celebrities fall. No matter how much we love them, everyone loves a good scandal more. And now Sherlock, the man who seemed to know everything, who could solve cases like magic, who was superior to everyone else in the room . . . now that man is nothing but a con artist and a liar. He's not superhuman, he's just ordinarily corrupt.

However, where Moriarty works alone, Sherlock has friends. Moriarty sees them as a disadvantage, as does Mycroft. But it's these friends who help Sherlock kick his addictions, who give him an apartment in which to live, who shoot cab drivers trying to give him poison pills, who put up with his arrogance, who pick up the groceries for him, who pay people to watch and protect him, who love him. (Yes, they often loathe him as well, but they mostly love him.) If season one was about Sherlock and John getting to know one another, season two is about the humanization of Sherlock. Through examinations of love and fear, we see that, despite his protestations to the contrary, he is *not* a sociopath but a human being who has trouble social-izing. He is capable of love and fear, of apologizing to friends, and of caring about them. When a thug beat Mrs. Hudson and put a gun to her head, Sherlock's retribution was swift and violent. When Moriarty strapped a bomb onto John, Sherlock was willing to do whatever it took to save his friend's life. When he realized he had humiliated Molly Hooper beyond reason, he immediately became humble, apologized, and kissed her on the cheek. Aside from the occasional hiccup, he seems to be trying harder with her this season than before.

No one has been humiliated by Sherlock worse than Molly has, and yet in this episode she continues to stand by him. No longer fawning over him, this quiet, shy person is the one who meekly deduces Sherlock, silencing him in the process. Sherlock constantly tells everyone that they *see* but they don't *observe*. Molly steps up and surprises Sherlock with her declaration that she has been observing him, and notices that he looks sad when he thinks no one is looking at him. She draws a connection between Sherlock and her father, who acted the same way, and when Sherlock counters with *"You* can see me," she quickly brushes him off, saying, "I don't count." Sherlock is speechless and looks at her like she matters for the first time. It's as if he thought Molly was a speck of lint that he kept trying to sweep off his exquisitely tailored coat and now he realizes she's actually a thread that helps hold that coat together. Her assertion not only shows Sherlock that he has underestimated her, but it also says something about his own personality: he's willing to put up a positive front for the sake of his friends and slumps into sadness only when he thinks they're not looking. Molly offers herself to him if he ever needs her, immediately editing her statement in case he mistook her words for a sexual advance, then she leaves the room before he's able to say anything further to her.

So when he returns to her later in the episode, and he looks like someone who knows he's going to die, the scene is so much more powerful because of the earlier conversation. The entire scene is written to look like a man sexually propositioning a woman on the eve of his death, causing our minds to wander back to Irene Adler's question in "A Scandal in Belgravia": "If it was the end of the world, if this was the very last night, would you have dinner with me?" Sherlock now believes this could be his very last night, and he appears to be asking Molly to "have dinner" with him. In the season two premiere, he told Irene, "I imagine John Watson thinks love's a mystery to me but the chemistry is incredibly simple, and very destructive." In "The Reichenbach Fall," he's not propositioning Molly for sex, but telling her that he truly does love her as a friend, and notices her, and that she means a lot to him. And that assertion from him probably means more to her than any tumble in the sheets. Like Sherlock's other friends (and despite Sherlock's protestations to the contrary in "The Hounds of Baskerville," the word is plural in his case), Molly cares for him and wants to help him in any way she can.

And so, when his friends' lives are threatened, Sherlock first comes up with a way to save them as he stands on the rooftop and faces Moriarty. And when that solution is taken away from him in shockingly graphic fashion, he's forced to do the only thing he can: sacrifice himself to save them.

In "The Final Problem," the story this episode is based on, Holmes and Moriarty fight to the death over the Reichenbach Falls, and just before falling to his (apparent) death, Holmes pauses to write a goodbye note to Watson. It's rather formal and gives him the whereabouts of a report that will help convict Moriarty's gang, but he also expresses his regret that his death will no doubt bring Watson much pain. Watson is not by Holmes's side because he has been called away to see a sick woman (as a trick by Moriarty), and Holmes confesses that he suspected the call was a fraud, but he let him go anyway to spare Watson from seeing Holmes die. In "The Reichenbach Fall," Sherlock is the one who plants the fake alarm over Mrs. Hudson and forces John away from the scene, but when John returns — as Sherlock no doubt knew he would — Sherlock calls him and says goodbye over the phone. "This phone call, it's my note," Sherlock tells him in a nod to the original story. "It's what people do, don't they? Leave a note?" What happens next is so shocking, fans were exchanging theories for the next *two years* waiting for the solution to be revealed in the season three premiere. The three themes of the season come together when Sherlock's love for his friends allows him to overcome the fear of death.

Martin Freeman gives a tour de force performance in this episode. First, in the opening scene, as he sits in his therapist's office several months after Sherlock's death and can barely speak the words; then, as he flips through the materials that Kitty hands him at her flat, his mind racing about what all of this new information could mean; third, the way he reacts to Sherlock's threat of suicide and actual jump; and finally, his total heartbreak standing beside Sherlock's grave. Freeman has shown us time and again what a titanic dramatic actor he is. If we could sum up in one word who John was before he met Sherlock, it would be *lonely*. The strains of "Watson's Theme" play whenever he fears being alone or abandoned again, returning to a dull life without Sherlock. And at Sherlock's grave, he acknowledges that. "I was so alone and I owe you so much," he says, with one hand on the tombstone. He is so utterly wonderful in this scene, stammering through his words, fighting back tears while expressing his deepest sorrow to a friend who is gone. He is broken. But he will not become the John that he was before Sherlock. Perhaps Sherlock has shown him there is more to life for him, and he will go out and seek it.

But without Sherlock, it won't be half as exci—
Waitaminute . . . who's standing behind that tree?

HIGHLIGHT John reassuring Sherlock that he believes he's the real deal: "Well, nobody could fake being such an annoying dick *all* the time."

DID YOU NOTICE?

- The discussion that John and Sherlock have about the deerstalker is hilarious, because for the past 100 years, most people have simply referred to it as a Sherlock Holmes hat, which is what John angrily calls it. Sherlock's bafflement at the hat's real name — "You stalk a deer with a hat? What are you going to do, throw it? Some sort of death frisbee?" — is one of the comic highlights of the episode.

- John tells Sherlock to lay low and take on a small case. Sherlock actually listens to him (which is worthy of mention on its own) and looks into a very old case (see below) where he concludes that Henry Fishguard didn't actually commit suicide. Hmm . . .

- When Moriarty writes SHERLOCK on the glass, he puts a little happy face inside the O that matches the happy face Sherlock painted onto the wall of his flat.

- Usually *Sherlock* uses only instrumental music composed specifically for the show, but in this episode they experiment with some great music. When Moriarty steals the Crown Jewels, he's listening to Rossini's "Thieving

Magpie Overture" ("La Gazza Ladra"); during the newspaper montage, you can hear "Sinnerman" by Nina Simone; and at Sherlock's apartment, the detective plays Bach's "Sonata #1 in G Minor" for Moriarty.

- During the montage of newspaper articles covering Moriarty's criminal trifecta, the *Guardian* article amusingly begins, "In a twist worthy of a Conan Doyle novella, Mr. Sherlock Holmes was yesterday revealed to be an expert witness at the trial of 'Jim' Moriarty."

- When Moriarty visits Sherlock in his apartment, he refers to Bach as "Johann Sebastian," similar to the way *A Clockwork Orange*'s Alex — a man capable of horrific crimes — would always refer to "Ludwig Van" instead of saying "Beethoven."

- Moriarty's "I . . . owe . . . you" message to Sherlock is repeated three times in the episode. It's cut into the side of the apple, then it appears in the windows of the office building across from Scotland Yard. Those ones are obvious. But when Sherlock and John are in handcuffs and running from the police, watch when Sherlock points the gun at John's head: you can see IOU graffitied onto the side of the building behind them, with wings painted around it. The repetition of the letters and words — as if leading to a revelation that never happens by the episode's end — caused fans to speculate over its meaning almost as much as they theorized about how Sherlock would evade death. Theories abounded on the assumption that all would be revealed in the season three premiere, and my personal favorite was one by fan Eva Christine (eva-christine.tumblr.com) who posited that the I, O, and U stood for iodine, oxygen, and uranium, because Sherlock mumbles "I.O.U." under his breath when he's in the lab with Molly. The atomic numbers for each are 53, 8, and 92. If one looks at the copy of *Grimm's Fairy Tales* that is found at the school, the 53rd fairy tale is "Little Snow-White" (featuring the queen giving Snow White a fatal apple); number eight is "The Strange Musician," where a violinist outsmarts a fox (Moriarty is wearing a fox tie-pin when Sherlock plays the violin); and number 92 is "The King of the Golden Mountain," about a boy who becomes king by undergoing several trials and succeeding (picture Moriarty sitting on the throne with a crown). Her theory was utterly brilliant . . . and never actually happened on the series. Check out her full explanation anyway, if only to fall in love with internet fandom all over again.

- So what *does* the "I owe you" refer to? In the end, it's possibly just a simple explanation: when Moriarty says it to Sherlock, he means it in a negative way — I didn't kill you poolside, so now I owe you a death, and I'm coming for you. That's contrasted with John standing by Sherlock's grave at the end of the episode, telling Sherlock, "I owe you so much." He means the same three words in a loving, positive way. Why does Sherlock mutter it under his breath in the lab? I believe it has less to do with the chemicals under the microscope, and more to do with the person standing next to him at the time.

- After the scuffle at the Diogenes Club (see "From ACD to BBC" below), Mycroft says to John, "They don't want a repeat of 1972." The way Mark Gatiss delivers the line is hilarious, and there's probably no further meaning behind that particular date than his insinuation that something *terrible* happened that year (there was probably a stale scone on the tea tray). However, 1972 was a year of great strife in England, with the miner's strike, Bloody Sunday and several other fatal IRA attacks, the crash of British Airways Flight 548 (with 118 casualties), ballooning unemployment figures matched with increasing inflation, and the premiere of soap opera *Emmerdale*. It was inevitable someone in the Diogenes Club would snap.

- The close-up of Richard Brook's CV not only states that his photo was taken by Arwel Jones (who is the production designer and art director on *Sherlock*, *Doctor Who*, and several other BBC shows), but shows Richard's home phone number and email address (Richard@r-brook.co.uk). It also states that he studied at the BADC (British Academy of Dramatic Combat), which is a real academy, and a superb detail.

- On the wall of Kitty's flat are the words "MAKE BELIEVE" in big letters.

- When Sherlock and Moriarty name Sherlock's friends, neither one of them mentions Mycroft.

- As John finishes his speech at Sherlock's graveside, he pivots on his heel before walking away, as if he'd just been speaking to a soldier.

- The creators of the show reveled in the theories that ran rampant around the internet, and ended up using a few of them in a webisode that preceded season three (see "Many Happy Returns" sidebar) and in "The Empty Hearse." Steven Moffat began teasing the fans, telling them that despite the dozens of well-thought-out theories, everyone had missed one giant clue. So what was it? It's still not completely clear, but knowing the reveal we get in "The Empty Hearse," I would guess that one should pay attention to the names that Moriarty rattles off as Sherlock's closest friends, and who Sherlock himself lists as his closest friends when he's talking to John. Sherlock says a name that Moriarty doesn't.

FROM ACD TO BBC Moriarty's repetition of "the final problem" is a nod to the story of the same title, from which much of this episode is taken.

- Just as this episode opens and closes with John's sadness, Watson opens and closes "The Final Problem" with a tribute to his friend. He explains that he's writing the story two years after Holmes died because he found the situation — "that event which has created a void in my life which the lapse of two years has done little to fill" — too painful to put into words, and is doing so now only because Moriarty's brother is publishing letters saying his brother was innocent, just as Moriarty tries to make himself an innocent in this episode.

- On the witness stand, Sherlock says, "James Moriarty isn't a man at all — he's a spider; a spider at the center of a web — a criminal web with a thousand threads and he knows precisely how each and every single one of them dances." When Holmes is describing his arch-enemy to Watson, he describes him similarly: "He sits motionless, like a spider in the centre of its web, but that web has a thousand radiations, and he knows well every quiver of each of them. He does little himself. He only plans."

At the very beginning of "The Reichenbach Fall," Sherlock is credited with Peter Ricoletti's capture. In "The Musgrave Ritual," Holmes is recounting some of their problem cases, and mentions "Ricoletti of the club-foot, and his abominable wife" among them.

When Sherlock is making deductions about Kitty, he looks at her wrist and says, "Those marks on your forearm: edge of a desk. You've been typing in a hurry, probably." In "A Case of Identity," Holmes similarly notices a woman's wrist: "The double line a little above the wrist, where the typewritist presses against the table, was beautifully defined."

When Lestrade is being interrogated by the superintendent, he says he's not the only senior officer who regularly used Sherlock, and that Gregson did also. Gregson was the other main detective in the Sherlock Holmes stories; perhaps he'll play a part on the series soon.

Although we caught a quick glimpse of it in "The Hounds of Baskerville," we finally see the inside of the Diogenes Club in this episode. In "The Greek Interpreter," when we are first introduced to Mycroft, Watson and Holmes visit him at the Diogenes Club. It's described as a place where the introverts of London, who hate social contact but want to get out of their houses, developed a society where they could go and read in peace. Holmes describes it as a place that "now contains the most unsociable and unclubable men in town," and then admits he quite likes it there himself. There's a strict no-talking rule in the club, because introverts don't exactly react well to conversation. That's why John gets hauled out of the room for talking.

When investigating the boarding school kidnappings, Sherlock is able to draw several conclusions from the footprints in the hallway. In several stories, Holmes looks at footprints and sees them as being just as telling as fingerprints: he is often able to deduce height, gait, gender, and other characteristics.

The boarding school case is taken from "The Adventure of the Priory School," where a wealthy student similarly goes missing and Holmes follows trails of tire tracks to find him.

While investigating the disappearance at the boarding school, the clue that John finds is a book of fairy tales by the Brothers Grimm. In "The Adventure of the Sussex Vampire,"

Holmes receives a letter forwarding him a case involving vampirism, and he says to Watson, "We seem to have been switched on to a Grimms' fairy tale."

On Richard Brook's CV, it says he's represented by the Mountford Agency. Lord Mountford is a character in Sir Arthur Conan Doyle's non-Sherlockian short story "An Impression of the Regency." Also, the press clipping inside states that Richard is soft-spoken, which is how Moriarty is described in "The Final Problem."

Mrs. Hudson talking graveside about all of the problems Sherlock caused for her is backed by Watson in "The Adventure of the Dying Detective," where he describes Mrs. Hudson as a "long-suffering woman" and notes that Holmes's "incredible untidiness, his addiction to music at strange hours, his occasional revolver practice within doors, his weird and often malodorous scientific experiments, and the atmosphere of violence and danger which hung around him made him the very worst tenant in London."

Moriarty manages to convince people that Sherlock is indeed the arch-criminal based on the extraordinary knowledge he shows in various cases. In "The Adventure of Charles Augustus Milverton," Holmes says to Watson, "I don't mind confessing to you that I have always had an idea that I would have made a highly efficient criminal."

INTERESTING FACTS

- The word nemesis is often taken to mean one's archenemy, someone who thwarts the hero's every move. But the word has a stronger meaning than that, and actually extends back to Greek mythology. Nemesis was worshipped as the goddess of revenge and divine retribution, especially against those who showed hubris. Sherlock's pride is one of his key flaws, and he demands a foe with equal arrogance to be his true nemesis.

- When Moriarty gets to the Tower of London, there are several shots of the ravens. The Tower of London ravens are in captivity, with their wings clipped, and they are protected by the British government (at the insistence of Charles II). Legend has it that if the ravens leave the Tower, the kingdom of England shall fall. There are seven ravens at the Tower (six requisite birds and one spare), and some have gotten away, or have been "fired" for being naughty birds, and in October 2013 a fox killed two of them, causing increased security at the Tower.

- During the newspaper montage, the author of the first two *Daily Express* articles is the fictional Aileen Hickey, who also had the byline of the *Daily Express* article announcing the death of James Phillimore in "A Study in Pink." The author of the *Guardian* article is Janette Owen, the real-life media and technology editor at the paper.

- When Sherlock is looking into the Henry Fishguard case, he says that the Bow Street Runners missed everything. Not only is this a quiet case, but it's a *really old* one that predated even the literary Holmes. The Bow Street Runners is the slang term for London's first professional police force, formed in the mid-18th century. Since the force disbanded in 1839, it's no wonder a cloud of dust flies into the air when Sherlock closes his casebook.

- The Diogenes club is named after Diogenes of Sinope, a Greek philosopher who was one of the founders of Cynicism. The Cynics believed one shouldn't have material possessions and should instead live in virtue, an irony that was not lost on Doyle, who described the club as a place filled with wealthy and important patrons. Diogenes was the most extreme member of the group, who lived in a tub in the street and relied on the charity of others. Based on some of the more extreme stories about him — involving him plucking chickens to prove a point against Plato, or publicly mocking Alexander the Great — he was either mentally ill or utterly brilliant, or both.

NITPICKS

- The opening montage of Sherlock being praised for the crimes he's solved runs counter to the character of Sherlock Holmes, who always worked behind the scenes and handed off credit to others. In the books, Lestrade and the other police at Scotland Yard always took credit, and Watson was frustrated that Holmes didn't. On the show, it's often mentioned that he doesn't take credit, so this montage seems contradictory.

- Richard Brook's CV says he is best known for appearing on the long-running BBC drama *Emergency*. Unless Moriarty actually did do several appearances on the fictional show — and if he did, actually showing John pop the DVD in to see him would have been the perfect way to show just how in-depth his con had been — anyone with access to the series could have found the flaw in that story right away.

- A close-up of the story about Richard Brook that Kitty will be running in the paper has the same couple of paragraphs repeated over and over again, but that's not so much a mistake as a typical way of doing props. However, in the digital age where fans can freeze-frame so easily, it might be time to start writing full articles.

OOPS

- In the *Guardian* article, the deck states that Sherlock would be an expert witness in the "Moriarty trail" [*sic*].
- There's an issue with the timing of this episode. We open with John crying in his therapist's office, and after the title credits we are flashed back to "Three months earlier." Then we see a few weeks of Sherlock being feted after solving various crimes, leading up to Moriarty's heist. At the trial, the judge mentions that it's been six weeks since the incident. Then, when John tries to use his card at a bank machine, it's two months after *that*, which is impossible, because following this logic, it's already a month past when John should have been crying over Sherlock's death in the therapist's office.

SHERLOCKIANS WEIGH IN
Charles Prepolec

Charles V. Prepolec is the editor of five Sherlock Holmes anthologies, including the Gaslight Sherlock Holmes series for EDGE SF&F. An active Sherlockian for more than 25 years, he was designated a Master Bootmaker in 2006 by Canada's national Sherlock Holmes society. Recent publications include Beyond Rue Morgue: Further Tales of Edgar Allan Poe's 1st Detective *(Titan Books, 2013) and* Professor Challenger: New Worlds, Lost Places *(EDGE SF&F, 2015).*

Do you think *Sherlock* is a faithful interpretation of the characters of Watson and Holmes? Why or why not?
Moffat and Gatiss have done the unthinkable with their BBC *Sherlock* series; they've managed to shake off 100 years

of accumulated dust, as well as the perceived stodginess associated with the Victorian era, and put the characters of Holmes and Watson back where they belong, which is to say in exciting, contemporary, cutting-edge character-driven stories as Arthur Conan Doyle originally intended. Conan Doyle didn't write quaint little period-piece mysteries, he wrote vibrant adventures, and that appears largely to be what we have in *Sherlock*. The writers get the universal nature of the characters and have done a superb job in dragging them into the 21st century and making them relevant to modern audiences.

What is your favorite aspect of Steven Moffat and Mark Gatiss's reimagining of the stories? What is your least favorite?

The best element of the series is in the casting of the leads. Cumberbatch and Freeman are, without putting too fine a point on it, damn near perfect in their respective roles. They'd have made a fine Holmes and Watson had they been cast in a more traditional period take on the stories, but that they are equally excellent in a series without the usual trappings shows just how lucky, or canny, Moffat and Gatiss were in their casting. Where the series has gone a bit astray is in executing their stories. There was a charming, almost tentative "dare we do this" nature to the first series that has since given way to a self-satisfied smugness and fan pandering which has been detrimental to the good works achieved early on. One can only hope that a fourth series is more concerned with good storytelling than lip service to the massive online cult fandom that has grown around the show.

What has been your favorite film/TV adaptation of Doyle's stories so far?

Picking a favorite Sherlock Holmes film or television adaptation is always a thorny proposition. Different productions have different elements of appeal at different times. Sometimes it can be about the actor playing Holmes, in other cases it may be about the look and feel of a production or in how cleverly an adaptation translates a story to the screen. When pushed though, I have to fall back on the 1987 Granada television adaptation of *The Sign of Four* with Jeremy Brett and Edward Hardwicke as Holmes and Watson. It happens to be my favorite Sherlock Holmes story, so I have a bias towards it, and the Granada adaptation manages to successfully bring all the elements of adventure, creepiness, romance, and general sense of fun that I love about the story to the screen. Of the BBC *Sherlock* series I'd say "A Study in Pink" remains my favorite to date, although both "The Great Game" and "A Scandal in Belgravia" are near seconds.

SEASON THREE (2014)
The Evolution of the Mind Palace

The third season is about how much Sherlock has grown and changed in the face of his humanization, and how people have learned who he is and begun to change around him.

This season has come under some criticism for its Freudian undertones, which critics argue weren't a part of the original books; but if a story is to be moved into the 21st century, human emotion and psychology are bound to take a larger role. The one thing the writers evolve throughout season three is Sherlock's mind palace, a place that has been revealed bit by bit over the seasons. And when his world changes through one significant event in John's life, Sherlock's control over that mind palace unravels, and it's only in building it back up again that he regains that control, with things becoming so clear to him that he commits a drastic act at the end of the season.

Sherlock has always been a man of intellect, leaving all of the sappy emotions and feelings to lesser mortals. In previous episodes, he has talked about personal connections being a hindrance to the greater intellectual games he prefers to play, but by slowly allowing people into his life, he's unwittingly become attached to other human beings. And yet, ironically, while these attachments are the very things causing a breakdown of the great mind of Sherlock Holmes, they are also what keep him afloat amid drastic changes in his life.

In one of the last Holmes stories, "The Adventure of the Lion's Mane," Holmes himself takes up Watson's pen and tells the reader that he's retired to a cottage and a life of beekeeping and, in his later years, that ordered "brain-attic" of his has become slightly disorganized. "My mind is like a crowded box-room with packets of all sorts stowed away therein," he writes, "so many that I may well have but a vague perception of what was there." On the show, this much younger Sherlock faces the same cluttered rooms, but if he's going to save his friends, he needs to reorganize them — fast.

On December 24, 2013, BBC Online released a webisode to promote the return of *Sherlock* on January 1, 2014. Featuring the characters of Anderson, Lestrade, John, and Sherlock, the seven-minute video showed the fallout of Sherlock's death on three of the people he left behind. Anderson is guilt-ridden and distraught and appears to have been let go from the force (as Lestrade leaves the pub he mentions that he'll put a word in about his case). By tracking odd events from Tibet to New Delhi, Hamburg, Amsterdam, and Brussels in the hope that Sherlock is out there somewhere, Anderson has become Sherlock and John in one, not only searching the clues and trying to map out Sherlock's return through his deductions, but giving names to each case and recounting them as if they're Victorian adventures rather than news events.

After leaving Anderson, Lestrade goes to John with some of Sherlock's personal effects that he found at the station. When he opens the box, we see a yellow mask, a pack of Nicorette patches, a toy replica of an L.M.S. Railway car, and a pink phone. The last is obviously from "A Study in Pink," the railway car could be a reference to the rail lines that Sherlock was investigating behind John's back in "The Great Game," the Nicorette patches were probably grabbed by the police during the drugs bust in "A Study in Pink," and the yellow mask could be a reference to "The Blind Banker," where a yellow cipher was written across a face in a painting. But it's more likely a reference to Doyle's story "The Yellow Face," a scene from which will appear in season three. It's the story in which Watson most overtly expresses the intimate relationship between him and Holmes. John looks like he's trying very hard to keep things together, and when Lestrade leaves, he puts on a DVD of outtakes of a video birthday card Lestrade made with Sherlock to wish John a happy birthday. It's at times funny and sad, and even though John pours himself a generous glass of Scotch to steel himself ahead of time, he's clearly moved, saddened, and angered by it. He mutters that Sherlock should stop being dead, and then we zoom in on Sherlock on the DVD making the final plug for series three: "I'm sorry I'm not there at the moment — I'm busy — but many happy returns, and don't worry, I'm going to be with you again very soon." *Wink*.

You can watch the video on YouTube.

THE EMPTY HEARSE

WRITTEN BY Mark Gatiss
DIRECTED BY Jeremy Lovering
ORIGINAL AIR DATE January 1, 2014

Two years after his "death," Sherlock returns to Baker Street after Mycroft tells him of an underground terrorist network that needs to be stopped. More importantly — and terrifyingly — Sherlock must face his friends who thought he was dead.

After almost two years of speculation and fan theories about Sherlock's faked death, the writers go with the intelligent option: don't commit to any one answer. Instead we see Anderson's loopy theory, parts of which are plausible, parts of which are fan service (crashing through the window and kissing Molly long and hard on the lips? Yes, please). We see Sherlock/Moriarty slash fiction (Sherliarty? Morlock?) come to life in the Empty Hearse meeting. And then we see Sherlock's version, which *might* actually be correct, but even when he tells a great story of exactly how it was done, Gatiss has already anticipated the audience response. He knew that regardless of what story they went with, the viewers would be unsatisfied and pick holes in it, and so they brilliantly add the little bit of Anderson suddenly pausing and nitpicking what Sherlock had told him. When Sherlock smirks and leaves the room, the insinuation is that what we just saw was perhaps *not* what actually happened. For all we know, Derren Brown really *was* there.

Regardless of how he did it, Sherlock lives, and with that

revelation comes a whole realm of complications, mostly with regards to the people most affected by his death and how they *probably* should have been let in on his little secret. At the beginning of the episode, we see a sobered John, quiet, no longer the "confirmed bachelor" that the newspapers declared he was in "The Reichenbach Fall," which clearly ruffled his feathers at the time. He's not the man he was at the opening of "A Study in Pink" — he's no longer alone, he doesn't walk with a cane, "Watson's Theme" isn't constantly playing when we see him — but there's definitely something missing. There's an awkwardness about him, whether he's speaking with Mrs. Hudson or Mary, as if he's lost some of his confidence. Perhaps where Sherlock always believed he looked smarter by standing next to "ordinary" people, John always felt more self-assured when standing next to someone with no social skills whatsoever.

This is an episode of regrets and apologies, where people discover they have inadvertently hurt someone else but were too caught up in their own miseries to notice. Anderson is almost mad with guilt over what he did, and we take a bitter pleasure in seeing him fall apart in front of Sherlock, begging for his forgiveness (apparently Sally Donovan is not similarly racked with guilt and, as we'll see in the next episode, is still on the police force despite Anderson being let go). Lestrade is as matter-of-fact as he always is, telling Anderson point blank that this happened as a result of what he and Donovan did, but that what's done is done and they all have to move on. We know he's missed Sherlock by his reaction to Sherlock's return, but Lestrade is either less attached to Sherlock than the rest of them, or he's really good at hiding his emotions. Molly, of course, already knew Sherlock's death was fake, so while she's been sad the past couple of years that he's no longer around, she hasn't been mourning him.

Mrs. Hudson and John, on the other hand, have been. We know that John doesn't like being alone, but the fact that Mrs. Hudson was constantly bustling in and out of 221B insisting she was not a housekeeper — while clearly being their housekeeper (who never dusted) — showed how much she loved being around the two of them. In the past two years, John hasn't contacted her, leaving her to grieve in the flat by herself. She's angry with him when he suddenly shows up, and even though the scene is laced with humor, seeing these two people bereft in the face of losing Sherlock is sad indeed. Their network had been dismantled (presumably neither of them has seen Molly); they've all become detached.

John is the most broken of all of them, which is why Sherlock's revelation in the restaurant is as cruel as it is hilarious for the viewers. In "The Adventure of the Empty House," Holmes returns from the supposed dead posing as an elderly bookseller, with whom Watson strikes up a conversation. When Watson's back is turned, so he can look at some of the books the old man is peddling, Holmes throws off his disguise, revealing himself. Watson takes one look at the detective and, not surprisingly, faints. Holmes is shocked and apologizes upon Watson's revival, saying, "I owe you a thousand apologies. I had no idea that you would be so affected." Our Sherlock is similarly blind to his best friend's devotion.

The scene of Sherlock's return in "The Empty Hearse" is so beautifully done because John is about to take the final step to divorce himself from his previous life. He's said his goodbye to Mrs. Hudson, taken one final look at the flat, and is ready to propose to Mary. Sherlock interrupts that last moment with a disguise that's meant not so much to conceal his identity as it is to catch John off guard. But John barely looks at him, making Sherlock's big reveal much more difficult than he thought it would be. When John finally *does* look up, he doesn't faint but looks like he just might. Martin Freeman plays this moment stunningly well, having John stare in disbelief for a moment, then clumsily stand up and hold onto the table for support, then hyperventilate with surprise, then with rage, and his first words to Sherlock are a complete struggle. Mary looks confused, and when it dawns on her who this stranger actually is, she shares in John's confusion, and her echoes of "You're dead!" punctuate John's heavy breathing and Sherlock's realization that perhaps this wasn't the way to handle the situation — "I'm suddenly realizing I probably owe you some sort of an apology."

Sherlock believes he can waltz back into everyone's lives so easily because it never occurs to him that his death would deal such a crushing blow to his friends. We see Mycroft's indifference to the situation, mostly because he knew Sherlock was, in fact, alive, but if that coldness was what Sherlock was used to as an emotional response, how could he have gauged that others would feel differently? Even the Holmes of the stories didn't anticipate his friend's reaction, but as soon as Watson wakes up, all is forgiven due to the fact that his friend is alive, which is all that matters to him.

This scene could have been infuriating for viewers, but it's saved by three things: the realization that among Sherlock's flaws is a complete ineptitude when it comes to judging human nature; Mary joining in the chorus by asking Sherlock repeatedly if he knows what John's been through; and the fact that John gets a few good punches in. In a wonderful series of subsequent events, we see them at a café (presumably having been thrown out of the fancy restaurant) and finally a kebab shop. The downshift in locations is akin to John moving from the life he tried to build for himself back to the life he had with Sherlock: each place is less glamorous than the one before it but more exciting, thanks both to the conversation and the amount of blood John draws from Sherlock.

Mary is a wonderful addition to the core group, adding an interesting new layer to the friendship: she's an outlet for John but she likes Sherlock and is respected by him, even if he regards her with some suspicion. Played by Martin Freeman's real-life longtime partner, Amanda Abbington, there's an instant chemistry between Mary and John that makes their relationship more believable — after all, they're supposed to have been together for a while when we meet her — and later in the episode we see her playfully teasing John in a way only longtime partners can do. When John worked and lived with Sherlock, he could only deal with Sherlock's frustrating behavior by rolling his eyes or giving Sherlock the occasional lecture, both of which went unnoticed by his flatmate. Now Mary provides a sounding board: he can talk to her about Sherlock, and Mary gives him an objective opinion rather than always siding with John. It's a much-needed evolution in how the friendship between the two men will rebuild.

Molly, on the other hand, has moved on, or so she says. Ever since her heartfelt speech in "The Reichenbach Fall," in which she showed Sherlock she was *observing* more than he realized, he's seen her in a new light. With John out of the picture and still fuming, Sherlock offers to make her his sidekick, and she comes along for the ride with her Tom Baker–like scarf and forensic knowledge. But when he surprisingly offers to buy her some chips, she pauses, unsure of what is going on; he's always turned down her suggestions that they socialize. She's learned her lesson and knows that Sherlock will never love her the way she once wanted him to, and that's when she reveals there's another man in her life. Sherlock nods towards her engagement ring, offering her his congratulations, but knowing what we do about Sherlock, it's obvious he already noticed that ring on her finger. In fact, it's probable that he knew she was attached all along, which is why he felt comfortable to ask her to be his ride-along: he knew there would be no strings attached. Louise Brealey is as delightful as she always is in the role, shyly stuttering through her obviously preplanned speech about moving on while still looking awestruck and smitten with Sherlock when he's talking to her. The reveal that she hasn't *quite* moved on when she introduces them all to Sherlock Lite, her fiancé, is funny, but it almost seems a little cruel to make her a laughingstock again, just as everyone is finally respecting her.

So now that Sherlock is back, he's realizing that things won't be the same. All of these people longed to have Sherlock back, but his long absence means that upon his return, he is no longer central in their lives. It's interesting to watch, in the next two episodes, how this new role as "one of the gang," as opposed to "the center of the gang," will suit him.

Like Molly, Mycroft knew all along that Sherlock was alive, and actually helped orchestrate the fake death, but now that his brother is back their relationship remains unchanged. In a brilliant scene taken right from the story "The Yellow Face," Mycroft and Sherlock deduce a man from the state of his wool hat, and reveal another tidbit from their childhood. Mycroft once again insists he's the smarter one, and Sherlock reminds him that he used to say that all the time, making Sherlock think himself an idiot throughout childhood. "*Both* of us thought you were an idiot, Sherlock," Mycroft retorts. "We had nothing else to go on till we met other children." And then, showing that Sherlock really *has* changed, he tricks Mycroft into admitting that he doesn't have to remain isolated and alone just because he feels different than everyone around him. In the season two premiere, Mycroft and Sherlock stood together outside the mortuary doors and talked about how they're different from everyone else because they don't need friends. Now, in the season three premiere, Sherlock not only *doesn't* see himself as being the same as Mycroft, but actually tries to convince Mycroft that friends are important. *Whoa.*

A lovely sequence shows us that John and Sherlock were meant to be together: we flip back and forth between Sherlock trying to solve an elementary case with Molly while John's reprimands ring in his ears (despite what we may have thought, Sherlock really *does* take to heart what John tries to teach him) and John watching the seconds slowly tick by as he deals with one monotonous case after another at his new medical clinic. Sherlock needs the comfort of having John by his side, lovingly keeping him in line, and John needs the excitement and danger that Sherlock brings. When John assaults a patient thinking it's another Sherlock prank, he realizes that Sherlock has gotten into his head. On his way to 221B Baker Street, he's attacked, kidnapped, and put inside a bonfire. Welcome back to your old life, John.

What works so well about this whole scene is that when Mary cleverly figures out a coded message sent to her — one that, as we will later see, was sent by someone who *knew* she would know how to decode the message — she immediately rushes to Sherlock. Mary could have been the extra, unwanted person in the Sherlock/John relationship, but instead, in this scene, she becomes Sherlock's ally in a race to save the person who means the most to both of them. In an instant, she goes from potential annoyance to fan favorite. Just as Moriarty strapped a bomb on John because he knew it would be the only thing to unnerve Sherlock, so too does this mysterious individual put John's life in danger knowing it would smoke out another person. But is it Sherlock he's trying to bring to the scene, or someone else?

Sherlock and Mary save John's life, but at the end of the episode, John watches his life flash before his eyes for the second time in as many days as he stands trapped in an abandoned underground carriage with only Sherlock and a ticking time bomb. By saving John's life at the scene of the bonfire, Sherlock makes up for disappearing for two years without telling John where he was, and they're back on an even keel. However, the dickish move at the end of the episode — where Sherlock pretends to be confounded by the bomb just so he can force John to forgive him once and for all — shows that some things will never change.

And that's exactly the way we like it.

HIGHLIGHT "Fffu—" "Cough."

DID YOU NOTICE?

- The main part of the episode begins and ends with John on the Tube: first riding it drearily on his way to Baker Street to face his demons, and secondly standing next to an active bomb. It's unclear which one is worse for him.

- When John looks up the stairs when he visits Mrs. Hudson, you can hear the sounds of "Irene's Lament," the violin song Sherlock played when he thought Irene was dead and she wasn't (clever!). You can also hear a snippet of conversation from "A Study in Pink."

- When the action cuts to Sherlock in a barber's chair reading a newspaper, the headline is "Skeleton Mystery," which points to the very case Lestrade puts him on when he returns.

- Sherlock refers to Mycroft as "blud," which is U.K. slang used in the same way as "brother" in North American slang, meaning someone who is very close to you. However, Sherlock probably means it sarcastically, given that Mycroft is actually his blood brother, but not really a friend. When Mary addresses Sherlock when they are first alone, he looks at her and we can see his mind palace at work. Several words swirl around her head, at first separate and disassociated — only, child, Guardian, Linguist, nurse, part, time, Shortsighted, Clever (this word flashes repeatedly), Disillusioned, Dem, Liar, Lover, Secret (this word appears only once), Tattoo, Lib, Cat, Romantic, Appendix Scar (seriously, how would he know *that*?) — and then the words begin to come together and some appear more often than others — Secret Tattoo, Cat Lover, Bakes Own Bread, Size 12, Liar Liar Liar.

- When the Empty Hearse fan group is meeting at Anderson's apartment and the news that Sherlock is alive drops, the BBC News ticker reads, "Magnussen summoned before Parliamentary Co[mmittee]." This will become important in the next two episodes.

- "Watson's Theme" plays at several key moments in this episode, but the most interesting use of it occurs when Sherlock and Mycroft are deducing who owned the wool hat left behind at Baker Street and Mycroft insists, "I'm not lonely." Listen carefully for strings plucking out the notes of "Watson's Theme" in a humorous fashion.

- Even though the word CAM is being used to indicate a security camera in the upper lefthand corner of the Tube surveillance videos that Howard Shilcott shows Sherlock and Molly, it's clearly there as a hint to the viewer who has read the books, pointing to the answer to the mystery.

- Mary knows what a skip code is and then handles herself really well on the motorbike when they're going down the stairs . . . as if she's done this sort of thing before.

- One of the texts Mary gets on their way to the bonfire says "things are hotting up here" instead of the more standard "heating up." While it's a common phrase in the U.K., it's unfamiliar to most on the other side of the pond.

- Sherlock's mother's prattle is hilarious and telling; while Sherlock is out solving mind-boggling cases, his parents are losing their keys and glasses between the sofa cushions.

- On the television, as the newsreader is talking about the all-night sitting of Parliament to try to push through an anti-terrorism bill, a commentator argues, "What freedoms exactly are we protecting if we start spying on our own people? This is an Orwellian measure on a scale unprecedented —" His point of view is an interesting one because it's not only one that Moran seems to share, but what Guy Fawkes was fighting against in the first place (see "Interesting Facts").

- Sherlock tells John that the only people who knew that he was actually alive were Molly, Mycroft, and about 25 members of his homeless network, but he's lying. Later we find out his parents knew, and then when Molly dumped the corpse out the window, she had two male colleagues helping her do it. One can only imagine how many other people besides John knew.

- The code that Moran enters to activate the bomb is 051113, which is the date, November 5, 2013.

- Sherlock mentions that he knew there was a corpse that looked just like him, so he had Molly look for it, and then he provided the coat. Perhaps this is what put the idea into Molly's head that there are other men out there who look like Sherlock. Could Tom be wearing the coat that Sherlock provided to put on the corpse?

FROM ACD TO BBC Parts of this episode are based on "The Adventure of the Empty House," which is the story Doyle wrote in 1903 that announced the return of Sherlock Holmes a decade after his death (and we thought two years was a long time to wait!).

- In that story, Holmes's choice of disguise to reveal himself to Watson is of an elderly bookseller. Like Mr. Szikora, the man in John's clinic whom John thinks is Sherlock pranking him, the bookseller is described as "a tall, thin man with coloured glasses." He drops a book called *The Origin of Tree Worship* (Szikora instead has a porn DVD called *Tree Worshippers*), and Watson picks it up for him. The bookseller tells him he has a shop on Church Street, just as Szikora tells John in this episode, and then shows him some other books — *British Birds* (which means something different in Szikora's saucy magazine with the same name), *Catullus* (a book of erotic poetry, which is probably what gave Gatiss the idea to make Szikora a smut peddler), and *The Holy War*, which is a titillating foreign film in the TV version.
- Holmes tells Watson that when he went to Baker Street to reveal himself to Mrs. Hudson (which he does before he tells Watson), it threw her "into violent hysterics," much as her scream indicates in this episode.

- Holmes explains, "I had only one confidant — my brother Mycroft," just as Mary says in this episode, "He would have needed a confidant . . ."
- Holmes describes what happened at the top of the Reichenbach Falls, and says he and Moriarty were fighting each other but he gained the upper hand: "I have some knowledge . . . of baritsu [*sic*], or the Japanese system of wrestling, which has more than once been very useful to me." In this episode, Sherlock begins explaining his 13 possibilities and says one possibility involved "a system of Japanese wrestling."
- Just before John headbutts Sherlock in the nose, the detective says to him, "You have missed this, admit it . . ." In the story, when Holmes and Watson immediately embark on their first case together after Holmes reveals himself to him, Watson writes, "It was indeed like old times when, at that hour, I found myself seated beside him in a hansom, my revolver in my pocket, and the thrill of adventure in my heart."
- Sherlock realizes the Parliament Buildings are going to be blown up by Lord Moran. In the story, upon his return to Baker Street, Holmes is hunted by Moriarty's right-hand man, Colonel Sebastian Moran, who is a sniper planning to assassinate Holmes after killing the son of an earl. When Holmes was dismantling Moriarty's network, Moran was the one person he couldn't prove had done anything until Holmes catches Moran in the act of trying to kill him with an air gun.

Throughout the entire Sherlock Holmes canon, Watson sports a mustache, which makes everyone's disgust with it in this episode even funnier.

In the second Sherlock Holmes novel, *The Sign of Four*, Mary

Morstan is a client who comes to Holmes and Watson to help her find her missing father. She is described as "a blonde young lady, small, dainty, well gloved, and dressed in the most perfect taste . . . I have never looked upon a face which gave a clearer promise of a refined and sensitive nature." Watson instantly falls in love with her, and by the end of the book she accepts his marriage proposal. However, whereas in this episode John becomes engaged to Mary, in the story from which this episode is drawn, "The Adventure of the Empty House," Watson mentions "my own sad bereavement," which many readers have assumed refers to Mary's death.

At the beginning of the episode, Sherlock is reading a London newspaper and snorts, "London. It's like a great cesspool into which all kinds of criminals, agents, and drifters are irresistibly drained." At the very beginning of *A Study in Scarlet*, when Watson returns to London from the Afghan war, he describes London as "that great cesspool into which all the loungers and idlers of the Empire are irresistibly drained."

In "The Reigate Puzzle," Watson mentions that in the year the story is set, 1887, Holmes had exhausted himself with "the whole question of the Netherland-Sumatra Company and of the colossal schemes of Baron Maupertuis." At the very beginning of this episode, Mycroft says Sherlock has been undercover by getting himself in deep with Baron Maupertuis. The "Sumatra" bit also plays into this episode (see below).

When Mary is reading from what appears to be John's blog, she's actually quoting *The Sign of Four*, where Watson describes Holmes's methods of solving a case.

Just as Sherlock's mustache jokes aren't welcome when he first reveals himself to John, the literary Holmes had bad comic timing, too. After making a bad joke to a client in "The Adventure of the Mazarin Stone" before quickly revealing the solution to the mystery, the client remarks, "Your sense of humour may, as you admit, be somewhat perverted, and its exhibition remarkably untimely, but at least I withdraw any reflection I have made upon your amazing professional powers."

Mycroft and Sherlock's deduction of the man based solely on his wool hat is a combination of three stories: "The Greek Interpreter," "The Yellow Face," and "The Adventure of the Blue Carbuncle." In "The Greek Interpreter," Watson meets Mycroft for the first time, and Mycroft and Holmes choose two men at the Diogenes Club and begin making deductions about their lives while Watson looks on, agog at the similarities between the brothers. In "The Yellow Face," Watson and Holmes try to make conclusions about a client using only his pipe (including that it has a sentimental value to the man, considering how many times he's mended it). In "The Adventure of the Blue Carbuncle," Watson and Holmes do the same using a hat, and Holmes points out that the hat owner's hair has recently been cut, judging by the hair-ends found on the hat. They also deduce that his wife has ceased loving him, based on the fact that the hat has not been brushed in a while. Sigh.

During the amusing cuts back and forth between John's office and Sherlock's flat, we return to Sherlock just as he's exclaiming, "Monkey glands!" In "The Adventure of the Creeping Man," a particularly creepy late story, Holmes and Watson get called in to the case of Professor Presbury, who has been seen creeping on all fours in the stairway and climbing the outside walls of the house, and his own dog has to be tied up because it's trying to attack him. Holmes discovers the condition has been brought on by a drug that uses the glands of a langur, an Asian species of monkey.

The case of the stepfather posing as the online boyfriend is an allusion to "A Case of Identity," where a woman receives a series of letters that turn out to be penned by her stepfather, also named Windibank. Just as Sherlock has some choice words for the stepfather in this episode, Holmes calls the man a "cold-blooded scoundrel." At the beginning of that scene, Sherlock sits next to the woman and pats her hand sympathetically while listening to her story. This is right out of "The Adventure of the Beryl Coronet," where Watson describes a client showing up who is distraught, and Holmes pushes the man into a chair and then "patted his hand and chatted with him in the easy, soothing tones which he knew so well how to employ."

When talking to the bookseller, Mr. Szikora, John determines that his regular doctor is Dr. Verner. In "The Adventure of the Norwood Builder," Dr. Verner is mentioned as the one who buys Watson's medical practice when he leaves to join Sherlock at 221B.

The note on Mary's phone — "John or James Watson?" — refers to the moment in the books when, as mentioned earlier, Mary refers to John as "James."

In "The 'Gloria Scott,'" Holmes is sent a skip code like the one on Mary's phone and determines that he has to read every third word of it to decode it.

John is shocked to discover that the two people Sherlock quickly ushers out of the flat are his parents. In the books, there's never a mention of Sherlock Holmes's parents. In "The Greek Interpreter," Watson writes, "I had never heard him refer to his relations, and hardly ever to his early life."

Sherlock refers to Moriarty's network as consisting of a bunch of "rats deserting a sinking ship," then calls Moran "the big rat," and finally discovers that Moran has hidden the bomb in a deserted Underground station under Sumatra Road. All of these descriptions are alluding to a single line in "The Adventure of the Sussex Vampire," where Holmes receives a note that mentions "the case of Matilda Briggs." Holmes explains, "Matilda Briggs was not the name of a young woman, Watson . . . It was a ship which is associated with the giant rat of Sumatra, a story for which the world is not yet prepared."

John's ultimate forgiveness in the face of certain death at the end of the episode echoes the words that Watson writes at the end of "The Final Problem," when he states that he shall forever regard Holmes as "the best and wisest man whom I have ever known."

INTERESTING FACTS

- Derren Brown is a British illusionist, mentalist, and hypnotist who is best known for his mind-reading tricks, demonstrated in TV series such as *Mind Control*, *Tricks of the Mind*, and *Trick or Treat*. He performs live and often uses celebrities as his guinea pigs, and he has done several sensationalized specials where he performs dangerous and incomprehensible stunts. Brown has been a friend of Mark Gatiss for years, and in Anderson's version of how he thinks Sherlock faked his death, Derren Brown is the man in the hooded jacket who comes up to John and puts him to sleep momentarily to reset his watch. He's a good fit for *Sherlock*, since he has written several books about mind tricks and how to improve one's memory, including directions on how to build a memory palace. Shortly before this episode aired, Moffat gave another nod to Brown in the 50th anniversary *Doctor Who* special, "Day of the Doctor," when UNIT covers up the Doctor's rather conspicuous arrival in central London as a Derren Brown stunt.
- The date of the unsuccessful terrorist plot coincides with Guy Fawkes night. On November 5, 1605, a group

of English Catholics attempted to assassinate King James I of England (who was also King James VI of Scotland) by blowing up the House of Lords on the day of the opening of Parliament. Guy Fawkes was the man in charge of the explosives, and he was the one caught the night before as he was guarding 36 barrels of gunpowder beneath Parliament. Fawkes, along with several other conspirators, was sentenced to be hanged, drawn, and quartered, a gruesome process that involved hanging a man until he was not quite dead, then disemboweling and beheading him, his body then drawn into four pieces. Just as Fawkes was about to be hanged, he leapt from the gallows and broke his neck, killing himself instantly to avoid having to endure the torture to follow. Since then, Bonfire Night, or Guy Fawkes Night, is held on the fifth of November in England, where effigies of Fawkes are burned and fireworks are set off in a show of patriotism. The tradition of carrying the effigy around during the day, as we see the boys do in the episode, asking John to give them a "Penny for a Guy," was to collect money for the evening's fireworks, but this tradition has fallen by the wayside in recent years, which explains John's perplexed reaction. Bonfire Night has traditionally been far more popular than Halloween in the U.K., but in recent years the Fawkes traditions are dwindling and more Britons are celebrating Halloween instead. Some of this has been caused by a turn in the emotional tide when it comes to Fawkes: donning a Guy Fawkes mask (made famous by the graphic novel and film *V for Vendetta*) has been popularized by the activist network Anonymous, and they are increasingly worn by anti-establishment activists at protests.

- Mycroft tells Sherlock where John will be dining that evening and adds, "They have a few bottles of the 2000 St-Emilion, though I prefer the 2001." Wine critic for the *Financial Times* and author of *The Oxford Companion to Wine* Jancis Robinson wrote a piece on the St-Emilion wines and explained that the 2001 was overlooked because it came after the popular and boffo 2000 year, but before the dreadful 2002 crop, but that the 2001 is actually superior to the much-touted 2000. We now know what newspaper Mycroft pledges fealty to, though he doesn't notice that he just declared the younger wine better than its older brother.

- The #Sherlocklives hashtag that appears all over the screen when the news breaks was one used in the BBC's social media campaign in the month leading up to this episode.

- The fantastic visual trick of making viewers think Mycroft and Sherlock were playing chess when they were, in fact, playing Operation led one innovative fan, Red Scharlach, to create her own version of what she thinks would be the perfect iteration of the game. Simply Google "Sherloperation."

- The man brought to John's clinic with a case of the piles is Mr. Blake. This is a nod to Sexton Blake, a multi-authored fictional detective first created in 1893 and modeled on Sherlock Holmes, right down to the facial features, housekeeper, sidekicks, and ubiquitous pipe. Originally created as a comic strip character, Blake has been the subject of novels, adaptations on the stage, radio, movies, and even a television series that ran for four seasons on ITV. In 2003, Professor Jeffrey Richards described him as "the poor man's Sherlock Holmes."

While Gatiss may have been making a snide comment about Blake by giving the name to a man suffering from hemorrhoids, it would have been funnier if the man John mistakes as Sherlock was named Mr. Blake instead.

- Sherlock's parents are played by Benedict Cumberbatch's real-life parents, Wanda Ventham and Timothy Carlton. Benedict later told *Radio Times*, "I nearly cried watching it . . . I'm so proud of them and I'm so proud of the reaction they got — and I think they're perfect casting as my parents!"

NITPICKS If Scotland Yard had scoured the room with the skeleton in it and failed to notice the easily opened trapdoor on the side of the desk, they really are as incompetent as Sherlock makes them out to be.

OOPS Sherlock's messy application of the fake mustache in the restaurant is suddenly perfect by the time he gets to John's table.

THE SIGN OF THREE

WRITTEN BY Steve Thompson, Steven Moffat, Mark Gatiss
DIRECTED BY Colm McCarthy
ORIGINAL AIR DATE January 5, 2014

Sherlock faces his most difficult task yet . . . when he's asked to be the best man at John's wedding.

"A wedding is, in my considered opinion, nothing short of a celebration of all that is false and specious and irrational and sentimental in this ailing and morally compromised world. Today we honor the death-watch beetle that is the doom of our society and, in time, one feels certain, our entire species."

This glorious romp might not be the most suspenseful of episodes, and is possibly the least Holmesian, but it certainly contains the most entertaining moments of the series. The dialogue is hilarious and the acting brilliant, as we join John and Mary on their happiest day, one that happens "offscreen" in the world of the books. (*For good reason*, Sherlock would say.) And yet, while the event is a celebration of the relationship between John and Mary, the episode acts as an examination of the friendship between John and Sherlock.

As with any big life change, whether it be marriage or the arrival of a baby, it affects two people the most, but then ripples outward, altering their relationships with other people. Both Mrs. Hudson and Mycroft ring the death knell on the ongoing partnership of John and Sherlock, which terrifies the detective. In the books, of course, Watson gets married, moves on, and continues to come back to Baker Street upon occasion for one adventure after another, with Holmes barely registering that he'd even been away. But this Sherlock is different — the relationships he's developed since meeting John have significantly altered him, as we saw in the previous episode, and just as he's awakened to the realization that people actually care about him, and he for them, he's about to lose the one he cares about the most. Or so he thinks.

By letting *emotions* (one can hear Mycroft saying that word with derision) invade what has always been a very clinical mind, Sherlock's mind palace is becoming cluttered and disorganized. In the previous episode, John's admonishments trickled through Sherlock's thought process and made him unable to complete tasks. In this episode, when John asks him to be his best man, the very suggestion — along with the implications of such an invitation — render Sherlock immobile. His mind simply shuts itself down completely, like a robot. In the face of the impending wedding, he obsesses over every single detail, as if he were the bride, and the wedding planning doesn't happen at John and Mary's flat, but at 221B Baker Street with Sherlock proving to be surprisingly adept at it. Perhaps he missed his calling as an events planner (or, from Janine's point of view, as a professional wedding guest).

On the stag night, everything begins well when Sherlock once again approaches the event in the traditional way — by handing over a one-inch-thick folder on John Watson's medical history to a chemist to determine the ideal alcoholic intake throughout the evening to avoid inebriation (don't all best men carry their own graduated cylinders to the pubs?) — but when John intervenes, it turns into a mess. Sherlock is hilariously drunken and slurring when he's "cluing for looks" on Tessa's case — Cumberbatch puts in a performance that's nothing short of Chaplinesque — and his mind is less competent than an ordinary person's under the same circumstances. For someone who relies on a mind palace where everything is filed away neatly, alcohol sends a hurricane into the filing cabinets and he can no longer distinguish between an egg and a sitty thing.

At the actual wedding, deductions come at him so fast he can't keep up with them, simply because he's not sifting through the information in his mind palace carefully, but finding it haphazardly. Twice he apologizes and says he has given "one more deduction" than he'd expected to. He falls apart during his speech when he suddenly realizes there's a Mayfly in the room, and the careful Council Chamber mind palace he'd created days earlier is suddenly unfocused, with a naked Irene Adler walking in as Tessa is frozen in her spot, and then everyone disappears except for Mycroft. Mycroft at first talks him through it, then raises the volume of his voice slowly until he's yelling at his little brother to FOCUS . . . and both mind palace Sherlock and actual Sherlock at the wedding smack themselves in the cheeks to knock Mycroft out of there, refocus, and figure out who the target is. In front of a large group of people, Sherlock can't talk out loud about everything the way he normally would and must put up a façade that he is simply giving a (wackadoo) best man's speech. Sherlock has never worried about what people might be thinking about him before, and a year earlier he would have simply remained rooted to the spot, talking loudly while everyone murmured in confusion around him. But now he's developed self-consciousness (once again confirming he's not a sociopath), because he cares about John enough to not want to embarrass himself and, in the process, John and Mary, by suddenly staring straight ahead and speaking like an automaton. And yet, he can't take John aside and run things by him, so he's instead left with a hostile and intellectually superior Mycroft in his head, berating him for missing the obvious.

Sherlock's mind palace has at times been over-the-top ("The Hounds of Baskerville"), beautifully stylized ("The Empty Hearse"), and funny ("A Scandal in Belgravia"), but its deterioration here gives us more insight into Sherlock's emotional state than any dialogue could have. It's a brilliant tactic on the part of the writers. Sherlock is falling apart both mentally and emotionally, because it's the end of an era, as Mrs. Hudson says.

The little chat with Mrs. Hudson at the beginning of the episode appears to be there for comic relief, but it sits in Sherlock's head and gnaws at him throughout the ceremony. That his brother uses the same phrase unnerves Sherlock — if Mrs. Hudson says it, he can easily shrug it off and send her out for biscuits, but if *Mycroft* echoes her words, then maybe he needs to be worried that this really is the end of an era. Mary and John sense Sherlock's concerns, and Mary coaxes John to convince Sherlock that despite the wedding, the game is still on, even if both men don't live at the same address anymore. But will it be?

This episode doesn't just look at the relationship between Sherlock and John, but is an examination of relationships in general. Sherlock deducing the men at the wedding and their dateability for Janine is just the tip of the iceberg — we see Greg Lestrade at the wedding alone (recall that in "A Scandal in Belgravia," Sherlock told him that his wife was sleeping with the PE teacher); Mycroft refuses to come altogether, being far more content with his solitary life; Mrs. Hudson appears to be with Mr. Chatterjee from the sandwich shop, indicating either that secret wife of his in Doncaster is no longer in the picture, or Mrs. Hudson has decided to look past it; Molly is with Tom, but watching Sherlock the entire time. No two relationships are the same, which is why Sherlock's education on the topic has been so difficult for him.

Sherlock is used to everything revolving around him. The only reason that Lestrade, Molly, John, and Mrs. Hudson even know each other is because of him. He's used to people dropping things at a moment's notice for him. The opening scene is a hilarious look at just how much Sherlock means to Lestrade and what the DI is willing to sacrifice for his consulting detective after having to live without him for two years. But it also shows Sherlock's utter lack of friendship etiquette, making Lestrade think he's in mortal peril when, in fact, he just needs help writing the best man speech. In "A Study in Pink," Sherlock barely knew John when he was texting him to come at once, whether convenient or inconvenient (he needed to use a phone and didn't want to walk down the stairs to ask Mrs. Hudson). But now he calls on Lestrade because he can't use John for this particular task . . . and also because even if he could, he's worried John would no longer come. John and Mary don't see why their relationship would change everything, but Sherlock does: he's no longer the center of attention. And with a baby on the way, he never will be again. The scene of the photographer asking Sherlock to please step aside so he can capture the happy couple is meant to be funny, but also meaningful: for the first time since they met, Sherlock has been asked to step out of a picture that involves John. Every time the media photographs Sherlock, John is standing by his side or slightly behind him. Now Sherlock's being asked to leave the picture altogether.

The mind palace's cluttered state suggests that maybe Mycroft was right in "A Scandal in Belgravia" when he demonstrated that Sherlock's relationship with Irene Adler got in the way of things, or in "The Empty Hearse" when he scoffed at the ridiculousness of friendship. But we also see changes in

Sherlock that are positive because of his friendship with John — the aforementioned cover-up when he realizes something bad is about to happen at John's wedding; his informal chit-chat with Janine that begins with him trying to impress her and get her a date at the same time, and ends with him telling her something private about himself; and finally, the way he's eventually able to disarm Major Sholto by telling him they both know he can't kill himself at John's wedding: "We would never do that to John Watson." This is not Sherlock making an emotionless, clinical appeal based on facts, but one that demonstrates just how much he's learned about human nature. Just one episode ago he was shouting "Surprise!" in a restaurant and telling Mycroft how "delighted" John will be to see him, completely missing the point, and yet here he talks a man out of suicide by appealing to his basic human decency. Understanding what his death meant to John Watson has utterly changed Sherlock. Even the hilarious notion of the jewel of Scotland Yard using his mind palace to offer dating advice to Janine is important: the deductions he makes about the men point to human nature, not just scientific fact.

If we had to sum up what Sherlock has gained through his friendship with John and the experience of returning from the dead, it's a sense of self-consciousness. He knows when he's being a jerk now. At the beginning of the speech, he confirms everyone's worst fears by first stuttering, then flipping through the telegrams as if they don't matter, then condemning the very institution of marriage before insulting John, Mary, the bridesmaids, the vicar, and pretty much everyone else in the room. But then he acknowledges that what he just did was wrong, that it shows a lack of understanding of what beauty or virtue is, before bestowing upon John the nicest things he's ever said to him. Suddenly, Mary is smiling widely, John looks like he's about to cry, Molly and Mrs. Hudson are dabbing at their eyes, and the guests are wondering why everyone thought the detective would be a disaster. (They'll soon find out.) His speech is heartfelt, and everyone can see Sherlock is *not* a heartless machine, but a man who has learned how to appreciate and even love his friends.

While Sherlock is very aware of just how different he feels, not everything he does in the name of Understanding Human Nature (wait for the monograph) is noticed. Sherlock tries his best to make it through the speech even when he looks crazy; he hates wedding traditions but abides by them anyway; his gift to John and Mary is a beautiful violin song dedicated to them that he performs in front of everyone; he tosses his boutonniere to Janine like a gentleman; and most importantly, he doesn't announce Mary's pregnancy to everyone but instead realizes it's personal information he should give only to them.

And then he leaves the party before anyone else, realizing the rest of the group is all paired up and the cheese stands alone. "I mean, who leaves a wedding early?" Mrs. Hudson asked him.

The one whose life just changed considerably when no one was looking.

HIGHLIGHT Greatest best man speech ever.

DID YOU NOTICE?

- When Sherlock is on the phone to Mycroft, he says, "What? . . . *What*? . . . *WHAT*?!" which was a characteristic reaction of David Tennant's Doctor on *Doctor Who*.
- While the reference won't be explained until the next

episode, when Mycroft says the word "Redbeard," he knows that he's triggering in Sherlock a reaction to a childhood incident that will alter the way he sees the day. This is one of the mind tricks that Derren Brown uses in his act.

- We get more clues in this episode that there's something about Mary . . . She sees right through Sherlock's fibs even when John falls for them; she ends up playing both men by convincing each one that she is in league with the other; and at the party when John says someone is going to die, she not only stays calm but rushes out to join the men and becomes an essential part of how they deal with Sholto. Also watch her reaction when Sherlock reads out the telegram from "CAM" that refers to her as "poppet" and adds, "Wish your family could have seen this." That will be important in the next episode. And finally, Mrs. Hudson's chat with John, where she talks about how her husband was running a major drug cartel without her knowing it, is full of foreshadowing.

- Tom suggests that perhaps Bainbridge had concocted a blade made of blood and bone, but his term "meat dagger" is what draws sniggers from people and the disdain of both Sherlock and Molly. And yet the ultimate solution was that the perpetrator used something akin to a meat thermometer. If they had taken him seriously, his words might have triggered the real answer in Sherlock's mind.

- When playing "Who Am I?" Sherlock asks if he's the current king of England, which is a nod to the fact that from Sherlock Holmes's resurrection in 1903 until the final story in 1927, there were kings on the British throne.

- The day after the stag night, Sherlock is Googling Major

Sholto and is reading an article about one of the angry family members. Written by Laurie Norris, the title of the story is "V.C. Hero — The Unanswered Questions: Why did my boy have to die?" and is an interview with Madeline Small, whose son Peter was killed in the mission that Sholto led. She claims that Sholto destroyed her family, that Peter was only 18 when she waved goodbye to him two years earlier. "He destroyed us all. And he gets a medal for it," reads the pull-quote. Peter is the younger brother of Jonathan Small, the photographer at John's wedding.

- When Sherlock realizes the Mayfly Man is at the wedding, he moves to "part two" of his speech and stutters, "I could go on all night about the depth and complexity of [John's] . . . jumpers . . ." John's jumpers, or sweaters, have long been a favorite thing to catalog in *Sherlock* fandom. There are lists and photographs and memes of John Watson's various jumpers, which have become an essential part of his wardrobe and character.

- Sherlock once again uses the "Vatican cameos" code that he yelled in "A Scandal in Belgravia" just before the safe opened and a gun began shooting people in the room. John finally puts speculation on the exact meaning of the term to rest here when he defines it as meaning "someone's gonna die."

- When Sherlock is trying to figure out the common thread between the women in his Council Chamber mind palace, he Googles their resumés to see if they all have worked for the same employer, and they haven't. And yet when he realizes who the target is, the link between the women is that they all worked for the same employer: Sholto. At first this looks like a mistake in the script, until Sherlock says they probably all had to sign confidentiality agreements, which would be the secret they refused to tell him, and why Sholto doesn't show up on their resumés.

FROM ACD TO BBC As the title suggests, many of the details of this episode are taken from the second Sherlock Holmes novel, *The Sign of Four* (originally titled *The Sign of the Four*).

- This novel introduces Mary Morstan, who comes to Holmes and Watson as a client because her father has disappeared. They eventually discover that her father has died and was part of a ring of men who had found a treasure and were going to split up the money until they were double-crossed. One of the men is the double-crosser, the other is the man who vows vengeance on him. Morstan simply gets caught in the middle and dies of a heart attack. Mary is owed the treasure, but only a small part of is it recovered. By the end of the story, Watson has fallen in love with her and they are engaged.

- The man who does the double-crossing is Major Sholto, and the man who vows vengeance is Jonathan Small, just like the two characters in the episode. Sholto has lost money on a gambling debt, and Small tells him and Morstan about the treasure. Sholto steals it, and Small vows revenge; he means to steal the treasure back from him, but Sholto inadvertently ends up dead. All of this happens before Mary even comes to Holmes and Watson, which means, just as Sherlock says in the episode, Major Sholto is already dead before he solves the case.

- Jonathan Small teams up with a diminutive Islander named Tonga, who shoots poison darts through a blow-pipe (Holmes accidentally shoots and kills him during a chase scene). In one of Sherlock's stories during his speech, he talks about a dwarf with a blowpipe.

- When Small is trying to steal the treasure, Tonga kills Sholto by shooting a poisoned dart at him, making him very much like the "invisible man with the invisible knife" that Archie suggests at the wedding reception, which ultimately helps Sherlock solve the case.

Mycroft is running on a treadmill and patting his stomach as Sherlock calls him, once again making a joke about the original obese Mycroft compared to the wafer-thin Mark Gatiss.

In "The Adventure of the Illustrious Client," Holmes states, "I am not often eloquent. I use my head, not my heart," and that statement could sum up most of the sentiments in Sherlock's best man speech.

One section of Sherlock's speech — "If I burden myself with a little help-mate during my adventures, it is not out of sentiment or caprice, it is that he has many fine qualities of his own that he has overlooked in his obsession with me" — is taken directly from "The Adventure of the Blanched Soldier," a late story narrated by Holmes rather than Watson: "Speaking of my old friend and biographer, I would take this opportunity to remark that if I burden myself with a companion in my various little inquiries it is not done out of sentiment or caprice, but it is that Watson has some remarkable characteristics of his own to which in his modesty he has given small attention amid his exaggerated estimates of my own performances."

When Sherlock mistakes John's question about who the best man he ever met was, he replies, "Billy Kincaid, the Camden Garrotter." In "The Adventure of the Empty House," the place directly across the street from the empty house is Camden House, and the killer — or garrotter — who operates from there is Sebastian Moran, Moriarty's right-hand man.

During Sherlock's speech, he mentions "The Hollow Client," which is not a case from Sherlock Holmes canon, although it could be a play on the title of one of the stories, "The Adventure of the Illustrious Client."

Sherlock recalls John watching a woman walk back and forth in front of their flat, clearly full of indecision. Sherlock says, "Oscillation on the pavement always means there's a love affair." This comes from "A Case of Identity," where it's Holmes who watches the woman outside and concludes, "I have seen those symptoms before . . . Oscillation upon the pavement always means an *affaire de coeur*."

Lestrade suggests someone tiny could have come through the air vent and receives only derision from Sherlock. However, his conclusion is both a reference to Tonga in *The Sign of Four*, who is a dwarf who comes down through a skylight window, and "The Adventure of the Speckled Band," which involves a snake crawling through the air vent to kill someone in their sleep. (And yes, it's as creepy as it sounds.)

In one scene, we see Sherlock stuffing handfuls of cigarettes into a Persian slipper, which is a reference to Holmes shoving pipe tobacco into a Persian slipper in "The Naval Treaty" and "The Adventure of the Empty House."

I hate to bring down the party, but while Doyle never explains how Mary died, many readers have speculated that she died in childbirth.

INTERESTING FACTS

- Sherlock says the best man he ever knew was Billy Kincaid. In the 1988 comedy *Without a Clue*, Ben Kingsley plays John Watson, a man who creates a fictional detective called Sherlock Holmes so he can write about the cases for which he's actually the private detective. He hires a man named Kincaid (Michael Caine) to impersonate the great detective.

- When Sherlock relates the story of the French decathlete found dead amongst hundreds of matchboxes, all empty except for one, John asks him what the final one contained and Sherlock opens it to reveal only a glow and a look of glee on Sherlock's face. This motif is an homage to several films that use a glow to indicate something so important it can't even be shown onscreen, such as in *Repo Man* (in the trunk of the car), *Pulp Fiction* (in the mysterious briefcase), *Kiss Me Deadly* (also a glowing briefcase, and the film Tarantino claims was his inspiration), and *Raiders of the Lost Ark* (the unseen contents of the Ark of the Covenant).

- When Sherlock is reading Bainbridge's appeal for his services, he mutters, "All the nice girls like a soldier," which John corrects to "sailor." They're referring to the traditional British song "All the Nice Girls Love a Sailor."

- Amanda Abbington revealed that drunk John Watson was very much like drunk Martin Freeman. "I loved [the stag night scenes] . . . He did stuff in those scenes that he does at home, or when he's mucking about. Like in the episode when someone says, 'Mr. Holmes,' and he points at Sherlock and whistles, that's my favorite bit. Martin does that a lot. Martin and Ben bounce off each other so beautifully."

NITPICKS

- For a man who couldn't tell a chair from an egg when he was drunk, how does Sherlock remember that Tessa used John's middle name?

- Sherlock refers to Bainbridge as a Grenadier, but the Grenadier Guards are the senior-most members of the Guards Division, and Bainbridge looks like he's more of a junior member.

OOPS

- When we first see the reception line, Mary and John are greeting an older woman in a pink dress and large white hat and a white-haired man in a light-gray suit. Then David steps up, and that same couple is standing behind him. As soon as he moves on, Mary greets them both again.
- Sherlock says that Bainbridge had a wound in his stomach, but we later see both him and Sholto being stabbed in the back, and when he's lying on the ground in the shower all of the blood is coming out of his back.

SHERLOCKIANS WEIGH IN
Peter Calamai

Peter Calamai, C.M., holds the investiture of The Leeds Mercury in the Baker Street Irregulars and is also a Master Bootmaker in The Bootmakers of Toronto. A veteran journalist and author, he won the Morley-Montgomery Award for the best article published in the Baker Street Journal in 2012.

Do you think *Sherlock* is a faithful interpretation of the characters of Watson and Holmes?

Yes. Too many people get hung up on the modern setting of the BBC *Sherlock*, yet the messages of the canon transcend clattering hansom cabs, pea-soup fog, and Victorian dress and manners. They are eternal: the misery that lies beneath the external shows of normalcy in many households, the conquering pull of true love and the jealousy that can accompany it, the desperate measures arising from greed, the sacrifices of patriotism, and so on. Above all is the eternal message of the profound companionship between two men who are superficially very dissimilar and their interactions with these and other themes.

To be meaningful to today's audiences *Hamlet* need not be staged by actors in Elizabethan dress on the open-air stage of the replica Globe in London. Reimaging Shakespeare's plays in a contemporary setting reveals their eternal messages afresh. So too for the canon. (Director-playwright Charles Marowitz recently demonstrated this point in "The Adventure of Sherlock's Last Case," *Baker Street Journal* 64, no. 4 [Winter 2014]: pp. 19–23.)

What is your favorite aspect of Steven Moffat and Mark Gatiss's reimagining of the stories? What is your least favorite?

I love the show-off cleverness of the script, casting, and direction. *Sherlock* never talks down to its viewers, unlike the American *Elementary*; it is a show about a detective while *Elementary* is merely yet another detective show. As well, *Sherlock* rewards Holmesians (the British term) with what the Japanese would call "fan service" — insider comments like the visitor counter on Watson's blog page being stuck at 1895. The secondary characters are superb — Andrew Scott as a maniacal Jim Moriarty, Lara Pulver as a nakedly scheming Irene Adler, and Lars Mikkelsen as evil personified Charles Magnussen.

I hate when important plot developments are conveyed by images of messages on the screen of a smart phone, unreadable on a 20-inch television set.

What has been your favorite screen adaptation of Doyle's stories so far?

I have many favorites. Like a baby chick imprinting on whatever it sees first, whenever I visualize Sherlock Holmes, Basil Rathbone is the dominant image. No other actor comes as close to the Paget illustrations. Yet for raw physicality it has to be Jeremy Brett, when he was healthy in the early Granada episodes.

The complex relationship between Holmes and Watson is captured best by Christopher Plummer and James Mason in *Murder by Decree*. The scene of Watson attempting to spear the final pea on his plate was rewritten at Mason's request to make it even more comical. For inspired directing there's Billy Wilder's *The Private Life of Sherlock Holmes*. Even the four Canadian films with the hopelessly miscast Matt Frewer can be admired for the authentic Victorian buildings (in Kingston, Ontario).

Finally, all Sherlockians look forward to seeing the restored 1916 silent film starring William Gillette, who could once again be recognized as the foremost actor to play Sherlock Holmes.

HIS LAST VOW

WRITTEN BY Steven Moffat

DIRECTED BY Nick Hurran

ORIGINAL AIR DATE January 12, 2014

Sherlock takes drastic action in an attempt to stop the tyranny of Charles Augustus Magnussen.

A stunning closer to season three, "His Last Vow" is the culmination of all of the episodes that come before it. John still has the same addiction to danger we first saw in "A Study in Pink"; John and Mary become another example of love leading to danger and heartbreak like in "A Scandal in Belgravia"; Moriarty is in Sherlock's head now as much as he was in "The Great Game," "The Hounds of Baskerville," and "The Reichenbach Fall"; Sherlock faces fear and possible death as he did in "Hounds" and "Reichenbach"; and Sherlock is haunted by his childhood in ways that were hinted at in "The Empty Hearse" and "The Sign of Three."

One of the major criticisms of *Sherlock*'s third season is that, for a show that claims to be a faithful adaptation of the books, it no longer conveys the same tone as the Doyle canon. Just as Steven Moffat came to *Doctor Who* and began exploring the emotional side of the Time Lord alongside the week-to-week adventures, some said he has decided to focus on the psychological elements of the Great Detective over his cases. Detractors said "The Sign of Three" might have been very fun and psychologically revealing and emotional, but was it Sherlockian?

Canonically, Sherlock Holmes is a man who is cold and clinical, with occasional sparks of warmth and humanity. Watson says of Holmes, "All emotions, and [love] particularly, were abhorrent to his cold, precise but admirably balanced mind." Doyle makes no mention of his parents, Mycroft is mentioned only four times in the stories (and there's a sense of rivalry without cruelty), and Holmes always stands superior to Watson. Watson looks up to him, even if he does so begrudgingly at times. Watson refers to their friendship with intimacy and affection, but doesn't make a big deal about it. Watson's marriage is barely registered by Holmes who continues working on cases; if Watson happens to show up, he takes him along with him, but doesn't seem to miss him if he doesn't. At times years go by where the men aren't in contact. When Holmes dies at the Reichenbach Falls, Watson is shattered, but when Holmes returns Watson is overjoyed and ready to tackle their next case immediately. He mentions Mary's death in passing and the men go off to help the helpless once again.

By contrast, on *Sherlock* the titular character is infantilized to the point of referring to himself as the child that Mary and John have practiced on all this time. John is infuriated by Sherlock's deceit when he discovers he's been alive for two years, and Sherlock must apologize to all of his friends. John's wedding affects Sherlock so deeply it shakes him to the foundations of his mind palace. He's constantly berating Sherlock for his inept way of handling social situations, and everyone around Sherlock tsk-tsks the great detective for not knowing the proper way to do things. In the stories, Irene Adler mesmerized Holmes but is rarely mentioned again and he encounters Moriarty only once; on *Sherlock* their presence looms large. Season three is certainly the season where the Holmesian purists had to either accept that Moffat and Gatiss were going to go off-book and create a new Sherlock for the modern age, or stop watching.

But what's so wrong with their approach? In the past 130 years, fans of Sherlock Holmes have read the stories over and over, have seen them dramatized in countless radio, stage, film, and television adaptations. And with only a handful of exceptions, they are set in the Victorian era with all of its necessary trappings. Moffat and Gatiss have moved Sherlock into the 21st century, an age where that which doesn't conform to society's expectations is labeled some sort of disorder; where anxiety disorder diagnoses are as common as the flu; where social media has opened up a world where people feel comfortable to share their deepest thoughts, feelings, and grievances either in a direct or passive-aggressive way. Of *course* in the 21st century, Sherlock would have to apologize for doing what he did. Did anyone reading the stories ever truly believe that John Watson's reaction to Holmes's return was genuine or realistic? Most people who have read that story, whether as a child or as a grown-up, react to Holmes's glib way of revealing himself with shock and disappointment, made palatable only by the fact that Holmes agrees he was perhaps hasty and apologizes quickly.

But now Sherlock is taken to task for treating his friends like that. Now we understand that such deceit can have long-term effects on relationships. Now we have so many terms to describe aspects of someone like Sherlock — sociopath, psychopath, Asperger's, autistic — that all of them are bandied about by one person or another. In fact, despite the past two seasons showing that Sherlock definitely does *not* conform to a diagnosis of sociopathy, he refers to himself that way five times this season, as if insisting that while he's starting to understand others' emotions, he still doesn't understand himself.

Moffat and Gatiss have made it clear that they're not just fans of the original Doyle canon, but of the pastiches and adaptations that it has inspired. There are shades of Rathbone, Brett, *The Private Life of Sherlock Holmes* (as mentioned, their favorite of the movies), the fake biographies of Sherlock Holmes (see below), and they even incorporated fan theories of Sherlock's fall into "The Empty Hearse." In the 21st century, male emotions don't have to be as stifled as they were in the Victorian era — even amidst that social climate, Doyle hinted that Watson and Holmes cared about each other deeply, despite their outward appearance, which in and of itself sparked early fan speculation. (Let's just say Mrs. Hudson isn't the first person to think Watson and Holmes might have been more intimate than the stories let on.)

All of Doyle's stories, with the exception of three — two told from Holmes's point of view, and the other as a third-person narrative — are filtered through Watson's perspective, so the television series gives us a chance to flip that narrative, look into the mind palace, and see what the great detective is actually thinking. Studies now show how rare it is for a child to have a genius IQ, but far rarer is a person gifted with extraordinary intelligence who doesn't also have anxiety, depression, or fall somewhere on the autism spectrum. Sherlock is haunted by an older brother who was clearly so jealous of him that he ridiculed him to the point of making him feel like an idiot all the time. When Mycroft appears in Sherlock's mind palace, it's never in a loving, comforting way like Molly Hooper; he's there to chastise him into focusing, to belittle him, and to remind Sherlock that his intelligence will always be inferior to Mycroft's. After being shot by Mary, in the last three seconds of consciousness, Sherlock goes to his mind palace only to hear Mycroft wasting his time by scolding him: "Mummy and Daddy are very cross." And in a funnier moment, the rivalry comes through once again when Mrs. Holmes opens the door and asks her two grown sons if they are smoking, and they both spin around like guilty boys caught with their hands in a cookie jar. Mycroft immediately lies by denying it, and Sherlock says, "It was Mycroft," like any annoying little brother would do.

One way Moffat and Gatiss have been delving into the psychology of Sherlock throughout the entire series — not just in its third season — is by showing the fine line between Sherlock and his adversaries. Magnussen is pulled directly from "The Adventure of Charles Augustus Milverton," and the episode stands as perhaps the series' best adaptation yet of one of Conan Doyle's stories. Despite Moriarty being called Holmes's arch-nemesis (mostly because for an entire decade fans thought he had killed Holmes), Charles Augustus Milverton is actually a far more nefarious and despicable creature, better drawn than Moriarty, and one of the only criminals who causes Holmes to do something illegal. In that story, Lady Eva Blackwell, a beautiful debutante, is about to be wed, but Milverton has letters that could compromise the marriage. Milverton comes to 221B and Holmes tries to hold him hostage when he sees one of the letters sticking out of his suit jacket, only to discover it was all a bluff. "Your supposition that I would bring the letters here in a notebook is entirely mistaken," the man tells him. "I would do nothing so foolish." Holmes decides to try something more deceitful and becomes engaged to Milverton's housemaid in order to gain information — to Watson's horror — and when Watson asks what would become of the poor girl whose heart he toyed with, Holmes simply shrugs it off. The two men find their way into Milverton's place — the Appledore Towers in Hampstead — but they're too late: Blackwell is standing before Milverton with a gun in hand, crying, "So you sent the letters to my husband, and he — the noblest gentleman that ever lived, a man whose boots I was never worthy to lace — he broke his gallant heart and died." She empties the gun into Milverton, and Holmes wastes no time in breaking into Milverton's safe to burn all of the other letters Milverton had in his possession before whisking Blackwell away and creating a phony story for the police.

Throughout both the stories and this series, there have been hints that Sherlock is just a sidestep away from being the criminal; whether it's the similarities drawn between him and Moriarty, or what he does under Adler's influence, or the suspicions of Anderson and Donovan, there's always a suggestion that given a push, Sherlock could have just as easily used his powers for evil instead of good. And here the revelation of Magnussen's mind palace aligns Sherlock more closely with him than with Moriarty. As Sherlock inconsiderately flashes the engagement ring at Janine to gain entrance to the building, he looks at John and gloats, "You see? As long as there's people there's always a weak spot," which sums up Magnussen's entire credo. Both men have the ability to name a perfume by sniffing the room; both retain information about people in their heads; both order their mind palaces in ways that allow them to access information when they need it; both are heralded in the British media as scions of their professions while retaining many foes; both prefer to stay out of the limelight on the one hand, while seeking attention on the other. As Magnussen is "reading" Sherlock's file while sitting in 221B and suddenly says, "Redbeard?" he unnerves Sherlock, then quickly snaps his brain back to the present moment and says, "Sorry, you were probably talking?" Just as Sherlock has the ability to put Mrs. Hudson on "semi-permanent mute," so too does Magnussen shut out everything that doesn't directly benefit him.

But Magnussen and Sherlock diverge in one key way: control. When Magnussen urinates in Sherlock's fireplace, John is revolted by him, but Magnussen's actions are different from Sherlock's social faux pas in that he is very aware of what he's doing, and his actions are carefully calculated. Sherlock, on the other hand, gets in trouble when he says something inadvertently harmful, unable to control other people's perceptions of him. Magnussen's mind palace consists of information stored neatly in the filing cabinets of his brain; Sherlock's mind palace stores the information in different spots, requiring a long string of mnemonic cues to get him to the one piece of info he might need at any given moment. He usually has to repeat something over and over again to jog his memory to its location in the palace, whereas Magnussen — as we saw at the end of "The Empty Hearse" — repeats the information over and over to himself to commit it to its proper place in his filing system right away, so it's easier for him to locate later. Sherlock needs quiet and isolation to properly access his mind palace; in "The Hounds of Baskerville," he shoos both Dr. Stapleton and John away so he can focus, and in "The Empty Hearse" he closes his eyes and somehow ends up on Shilcott's landing without realizing he'd removed himself from the company of others. Magnussen, on the other hand, simply requires his glasses, which — despite the visual trickery meant to con us into thinking the filing system *is* the glasses — act only as a ritual for him. He cleans his glasses, looks clearly ahead, and can instantly access his memory vaults. Magnussen is all about order and control; Sherlock's mind palace can become cluttered and disordered when facing stress, as we saw in "The Sign of Three." Sherlock is also easily unnerved when a situation involves one of his friends, whereas the friendless and bloodless Magnussen has nerves of steel.

That's not to say, once again, that Sherlock's friends are a detriment to him. Magnussen actually *does* lose control at one moment in this episode: when Mary is pointing a gun at his forehead. And yet, when she turns the gun on Sherlock, he maintains a cool calm. To be fair, Magnussen has every right to be scared — he knows what he's done to Mary and how easily she could take his life — whereas Sherlock assumes his friend would never actually pull the trigger. But where Magnussen is crouched on the floor, babbling in Danish, Sherlock simply stands there once the bullet has penetrated him, and Molly enters his mind palace. With the help of Anderson, and Mycroft's intermittent rebukes, Mind Palace Molly is able to help Sherlock fall in the direction that will buy him some time and prevent his body from going into shock. Aside from being a scene with the most stunning visual effects of the entire series, it's one that brings joy to all the Molly Hooper fans, for it shows that back in "The Reichenbach Fall" when he discovered she's reliable and discreet, he inserted her into his mind palace as the voice of reason, comfort, and aid. Mycroft has long been entrenched in that mind palace as a voice of abuse — but here it's abuse that tries to guide Sherlock as it lectures him.

While John isn't in the mind palace, he *is* the very person who will save Sherlock's life. Moriarty found his way into the palace when Sherlock first encountered him, but only as a specter there to strike fear in Sherlock's heart and make him think his life is in danger. Now that Moriarty's dead (maybe), Sherlock has placed him in his memory banks as a prisoner in a padded cell, filthy and drooling, chained to the wall like a dog but still taunting Sherlock. And as Moriarty curls up next to Sherlock's dying body — importantly, in death, Sherlock places himself forever in that cell rather than in any other mind palace room — he says the one thing that jolts Sherlock back to reality: "John Watson is definitely in danger."

Which brings us back to Redbeard. Clearly Redbeard was a childhood dog loyal to Sherlock, who came when he was called, who loved Sherlock for no reason other than the fact that he was Sherlock. For years Sherlock has been haunted by the death of Redbeard, placing him safely in his mind palace where he waits patiently for his young master to come and visit him. Sherlock accesses him when he needs shoring up. In the previous episode, Mycroft cruelly says "Redbeard" right before Sherlock's best man speech, knowing that it will unravel his little brother. John has become Redbeard for Sherlock, the friend who is loyal to him no matter what, who will always come back to him, the one he fears losing to Mary — first through marriage, and now through the new knowledge he has of her. He has been broken since losing his first loyal companion, and he's not about to lose another.

The neat twist of Mary Watson being a former intelligence agent gone rogue is a great way to liven up a character that Doyle just tossed into a corner after *The Sign of Four*, mentioning her in passing occasionally and quietly killing her off when she was getting in the way of further adventures. In an age where we like to see our female characters just as strong and capable and multifaceted as their male counterparts, Moffat and Gatiss have chosen to make Mary more than just a pregnant housewife who's the nurse to John's doctor, giving her instead a mysterious past, making her an excellent sharpshooter, clear-headed under pressure, yet still deeply in love with her husband. It's a testament to John that he finds his way back to her on Christmas after what she did. Despite the writers trying to move along quickly with the revelation by having Sherlock blame John for seeking out adventurous companions, that explanation — and Mary's complicity in it, where she goes along with Sherlock and basically says, "Yeah, it's *your* fault" — is immensely frustrating. John might crave adventure, but he also craves honesty. And he deserves better than what happens. But when he takes time to think, he realizes that if he could forgive his best friend for lying about his death for two years and forcing him to mourn needlessly, he can forgive his pregnant wife who did everything she did to protect him. When he sprains Wiggins's arm at the drug den, he demonstrates that he has some skills he hasn't told anyone about, too. Sherlock might be able to solve crimes like no one else on the planet, and Mary may be able to shoot out the center of a spinning 50-pence coin at six feet, but when it comes to putting others before himself in every situation, John is the true hero.

At the end of the episode, Sherlock commits a shocking act to save his friends, not caring about the consequences he'll have to face so much as the comfort of knowing his best friends will be safe. Again, detractors — who didn't seem to mind when John shoots Jeff the cabbie in "A Study in Pink" to save Sherlock's life — cried that Sherlock never killed anyone in the canon. For the most part, it's true: Holmes kills Moriarty, and both his and Watson's guns go off at the same time in *The Sign of Four*, which results in the death of Tonga, but both those instances were cases of self-defense. Couldn't Sherlock have deduced his way out of this? Perhaps. But throughout this season we've seen Sherlock's emotions overcoming his intelligence at times, as if, in his robot-like, studied version of humanity, he hasn't figured out how to both think and feel at the same time. He missed the signs that something was off with Mary, and he never guessed that Magnussen had a mind palace like him. He thought he'd come up with the perfect plan in pretending to bring Mycroft's laptop to Magnussen to catch him in the act — just as Lestrade says in "The Sign of Three" that the only way he could bring an end to the Waters family gang was to catch them in the act — but Magnussen was already a step ahead of him. He saw Magnussen cowering on the floor before Mary, and in that moment seems to deduce it's the only way out.

Holmes being brought to a murderous point over the safety of Watson is not something new to the canon, however. In one of the last stories, "The Adventure of the Three Garridebs," Holmes miscalculates the reaction of the villain who shoots at Holmes and Watson as they surprise him in a room. Watson takes a bullet to the thigh, and Holmes, horrified, rushes to his friend's side, begging him to tell him that he's not hurt. Watson reassures him it's just a scratch, and Holmes turns to the criminal and hisses, "If you had killed Watson, you would not have got out of this room alive." The bullet merely grazed Watson's leg, yet Holmes was so incensed he threatened murder. Here, Sherlock watches Magnussen humiliate John by flicking him in the eye, watching his proud friend have to take it, and you can see the rage rising within Sherlock. He is used to humiliation, but he doesn't take lightly anyone who threatens or hurts his friends. When Sherlock shoots Magnussen, John is beside himself with anguish at the sudden turn of events, but Sherlock comforts him by telling him he's reassured the safety of both John and Mary. Even in the midst of his torment, John looks at Sherlock in a new way, as if up until now he didn't realize what he meant to Sherlock. Similarly, as Watson looks at Holmes in that moment of Holmes sitting beside him in a panic, he thinks, "It was worth a wound — it was worth many wounds — to know the depth of loyalty and love which lay behind that cold mask."

On the other hand, Mycroft, sitting in the helicopter, only sees the small boy he used to torment. Just as Sherlock lives with the wounds of inferiority perpetrated by his older brother, so too, it seems, does Mycroft live with the guilt of what he did to him. The reason he continues to scold Sherlock yet look out for him at every turn (even admitting that Sherlock's death would break his heart) is because, to Mycroft, Sherlock will always be his baby brother in need of his lectures and assistance. And in this moment, Mycroft is unable to protect him. Magnussen tells Sherlock that by using the chain of loyalty, he was able to get to Mycroft through Mary. But in this scene, we discover that Mary's threat from Magnussen, which led to John's humiliation at the hands of Magnussen, led to Sherlock protecting both of them with Mycroft powerless to intervene. "My brother is a murderer," Mycroft says with much sadness at the end.

And then . . . Sherlock is gone.

And then he's back.

In the shortest exile in British history, a strange turn of events suddenly reverses everything that had been built up, and Sherlock's off the hook through some weird form of *deus ex machina*. Is Moriarty really alive? Is it a con designed to lure Sherlock back rather than sending him to his certain death? Could Mycroft have simply orchestrated the stunt? Whatever it is, Sherlock has evaded death once again . . . and when season four returns, the game will be back on.

HIGHLIGHT

Bill: They call me The Wig.

Sherlock: No they don't.

Bill: Well, they call me Wiggy.

Sherlock: Nope.

Bill: Bill. Bill Wiggins.

- Sherlock is angry with John for blowing his cover in the drug den, but if he hadn't turned around and said John's name, John would have gone on his way with Isaac and would have never seen him there.

- When John says he's going to make Sherlock pee in a cup, he sounds exactly like his American counterpart on *Elementary*, Joan Watson.

- According to Magnussen's file, Mrs. Hudson's full name is Martha Louise Hudson, she's a semi-reformed alcoholic who was an exotic dancer, has 21% debt, and her pressure point is marijuana. John Watson's pressure points are his alcoholic sister and Mary. In Sherlock's file, it says his porn preference is "normal," it confirms Mycroft does indeed work for MI-6 (until now it's just been speculated), and his pressure points are John Watson, Irene Adler, Jim Moriarty, Redbeard, "the Hounds of the Baskerville," and opium. Interestingly, Molly and Mrs. Hudson aren't there, and if Magnussen had been paying as much attention to Sherlock as he says he's been, he would have noticed his attention to both women.

- Just to reiterate, Sherlock's porn preference is listed as *normal*.

- In "The Empty Hearse," when Sherlock's mother is chattering on the couch at 221B, she says her husband is always losing his glasses and suggests he wear them on a chain around his neck. In this episode, we see that he took her advice.

- When Sherlock is dying, he stumbles down a flight of stairs that looks strikingly like the one from "A Study in Pink." However, close examination through freeze frames shows that the railings and configurations of the stairs are slightly different, so they're using a stairwell that evokes "A Study in Pink," but isn't the same one.

- When Sherlock sees Mary standing in the long corridor with the wooden doors in his mind palace, she's wearing the same outfit she was at the restaurant when he first meets her in "The Empty Hearse."

- We see Magnussen go down the stairs into his vaults and take out a photo of a girl and then put it onto his projector and stare at it. Now we realize the vaults are just in his mind, so he was simply staring at the photo to memorize it. In "The Empty Hearse," he's sitting in his vaults at the end of the episode watching a film of Sherlock and Mary pulling John out of the bonfire, but now we know he was simply playing a mental film over and over in his head in his empty room, not in the vaults as he appeared to be doing.

- Magnussen drops several hints about his memory palace throughout the episode: in the first scene at the parliamentary committee meeting, he says he has an excellent memory. When he shows up at 221B, he tells them this is his office, then John's stats run through his head and he adds it's his office *now*, as if the statistics prove he has his filing cabinets close by.

- In "The Reichenbach Fall," Sherlock investigates the old Henry Fishguard case and says that Henry didn't actually commit suicide. We assumed at the time that was a reference to Sherlock; perhaps it was also a hint about Moriarty?

FROM ACD TO BBC As mentioned, most of this episode comes from "The Adventure of Charles Augustus Milverton." Moffat sticks pretty close to the source material for this one, and Lars

Mikkelsen plays the part of Charles Augustus Magnussen with aplomb. With the exception of Milverton being clean-shaven and rather plump, they couldn't have found an actor who more embodies the character in Conan Doyle's vision. Like Mikkelsen, he is described as "a man of fifty, with a large, intellectual head" who exudes a sense of "benevolence," except for "the insincerity of the fixed smile and by the hard glitter of those restless and penetrating eyes. His voice was as smooth and suave as his countenance." Holmes is repulsed by him, and just as Sherlock tries to convey to John how horrible a man he is by likening him to a shark slowly swimming in an aquarium (which is largely unheard by John, who instead is marveling at the fact that he just saw Sherlock snogging a woman), Holmes describes him to Watson: "Do you feel a creeping, shrinking sensation, Watson, when you stand before the serpents in the Zoo, and see the slithery, gliding, venomous creatures, with their deadly eyes and wicked, flattened faces? Well, that's how Milverton impresses me. I've had to do with 50 murderers in my career, but the worst of them never gave me the repulsion which I have for this fellow."

In addition to the major points listed above:

- Holmes proposes to Milverton's housekeeper; Sherlock proposes to Magnussen's personal assistant. The detective's best friend is equally repulsed in both versions.
- Lady Eva Blackwell from the story becomes a combination of Lady Elizabeth Smallwood and Mary Watson. Like with Blackwell, Magnussen has letters that implicate Smallwood's husband in a scandal, and her husband commits suicide over it, as we see in a newspaper headline. However, Smallwood doesn't take matters into her own hands like Blackwell does — that side of the literary character is embodied in Mary.

- Just as Milverton keeps a notebook in his pocket that leads Holmes to believe he's brought Lady Blackwell's letters to 221B, so does Magnussen show Sherlock some fake letters to make him believe they're Smallwood's.

Sherlock refers to Magnussen as "the Napoleon of blackmail," but in the stories it's Moriarty to whom he refers as "the Napoleon of crime."

Sherlock in the drug den is taken from a story called "The Man with the Twisted Lip." In that story, Watson is awakened late one night by a neighbor who asks him if he could help her get her husband out of an opium den. The man's name is Isa Whitney (on *Sherlock* the boy's name is Isaac Whitney). When Watson goes to the opium den to extract him, he finds Holmes there, disguised as an old man and working on a case involving the den.

Just as Molly slaps Sherlock and says, "How dare you throw away the beautiful gifts you were born with?" at the beginning of *The Sign of Four*, as Watson is chastising Holmes for doing cocaine, he says, "Why should you, for a mere passing pleasure, risk the loss of those great powers with which you have been endowed?"

As mentioned earlier, Holmes makes great use of the "Baker Street Irregulars" in the stories, his name for Sherlock's "Homeless Network." Wiggins is the name of the kid who does the talking for the gang.

In dozens of stories, a trademark line of Holmes is to remind Watson to bring a gun. Here, for the first time, he distinctly tells John *not* to bring one to Magnussen's office.

John gaining weight post-marriage is from "A Scandal in Bohemia," where Holmes suggests he's put on "7.5 pounds" since marrying, and even though Watson insists it's only seven, Holmes sticks to his original proposition.

When Janine visits Sherlock in the hospital, she says she's bought a cottage in Sussex Downs. "There's beehives," she says, "but I'm getting rid of those." This is a reference to the fact that, as mentioned in three of the later stories, Holmes eventually retires to a cottage in Sussex Downs where he takes up beekeeping.

Sherlock leads Mary to Leinster Gardens where she discovers two "empty houses." In "The Adventure of the Empty House," Sebastian Moran sits in Camden House waiting to assassinate Holmes, and Holmes is able to sneak up on him by creating a dummy of himself in the window of 221B across the street, which he has Mrs. Hudson come and move slightly every few minutes, just as John sits in the empty house in this episode, and Mary takes him to be a dummy.

In *The Sign of Four*, the fortune that Mary Morstan's father was cheated out of is called the Agra treasure, because it was taken from the Agra fort in India. Watson worries throughout the story that if they *do* recover the fortune, Morstan's station will be raised so high that she'll never consider his marriage proposal. In this episode, Mary's initials are revealed as A.G.R.A., and if John reads the information on the memory stick that she gives to him, she believes it could keep them apart.

Sherlock's mother wrote *The Dynamics of Combustion*. In *The Valley of Fear*, Holmes mentions that among Professor Moriarty's many academic achievements was his brilliant book *The Dynamics of an Asteroid*.

Magnussen says that "for those who understand these things Mycroft is the most powerful man in the country." In "The Adventure of the Bruce-Partington Plans," Holmes refers to his brother as "the most indispensible man in the country."

Mycroft features more heavily in this episode than any other, probably because in the books he has the same brain capacity that Magnussen demonstrates in this episode. In "The Adventure of the Bruce-Partington Plans," Holmes explains to Watson what Mycroft does for the British government: "He has the tidiest and most orderly brain, with the greatest capacity for storing facts, of any man living . . . In that great brain of his everything is pigeon-holed and can be handed out in an instant."

The discussion between John and Sherlock on the tarmac is taken from the same story that gives this episode its title: "His Last Bow." In that story, Holmes and Watson are reunited after over two years apart to take down a German spy ring. Chronologically, it's meant to be the last adventure they have; written in September 1917, it's set in August 1914, on the eve of the First World War. After solving the case, Holmes takes Watson aside for a conversation, saying, as Sherlock does at the end of the episode, that it may be "the last quiet talk that we shall ever have." Then Holmes looks off at the sea and says, "There's an east wind coming, Watson." He's referring to the impending war, and the Germans being the "cold and bitter" wind that shall blow on England from the east.

INTERESTING FACTS

- As soon as Magnussen leaves Sherlock's flat, Sherlock rushes out to a cab and directs the driver to Hatton Garden. This is an area of London near Camden that is known as London's jewelry quarter, and clearly he's going there to pick up Janine's ring.
- Sherlock deduces that one of Magnussen's security guards is an ex-con and a white supremacist based on his tattoos, which are a number 14 behind his ear (shown first), and then a series of five dots placed the way they would appear on a die. They're shown in the incorrect order: the five dots indicate he's an ex-con by representing

the four walls and the prisoner stuck in the center. The 14 tattoo is a common white supremacist tattoo referring to 14 words from an infamous quote by white nationalist leader David Lane: "We must secure the existence of our people and a future for white children."

- Amanda Abbington says the show's firearms expert told her the gun she uses to shoot Sherlock was the same one Daniel Craig used in *Skyfall*. "I hope that's true and he wasn't just taking the mickey out of me," she laughs.

- Numbers 23 and 24 Leinster Gardens are indeed false fronts that contain no real houses behind them. There were once five-storey houses built there just like the other upscale houses in the neighborhood, but when the route between Paddington and Bayswater stations opened, the houses at these two addresses had to be torn down to open a stretch where the steam engines could "vent off." The façade was kept, however, with the windows darkened, and even some longtime residents of the area have no idea those houses aren't real.

- The boy who plays the young Sherlock Holmes is Louis Moffat, Steven Moffat and producer Sue Vertue's son.

- Sherlock tells John that his full name is William Sherlock Scott Holmes. This is not from Doyle canon, but is instead part of the much larger Sherlockian game that's been played by fans and scholars alike since the early 20th century, treating Holmes and Watson as if they're real people. Sci-fi writer Philip José Farmer often wrote several fictional biographies of literary characters. Now known as the "Wold Newton family" of books, the premise was that a meteorite fell near Wold Newton in Yorkshire in 1795, and some people going by in a coach were exposed to radiation. As a result, their descendants ended up with extraordinary intelligence and strength, and included such literary luminaries (all now related through this incident) as Allan Quatermain, James Bond, Sam Spade, Professor Moriarty, Nero Wolfe (who is now Sherlock Holmes's son), and Sherlock Holmes. After Farmer got the world started, others jumped in and began expanding the Wold Newton world, and not only was Holmes's name expanded to William Sherlock Scott Holmes, he was one of eight children, which include Mycroft, his sister Shirley, and Rutherford, his vampire twin. Obviously.

- Another result of Holmesian speculation was a fictional biography of Sherlock Holmes by William S. Baring-Gould called *Sherlock Holmes of Baker Street* (1962). In that book, he wrote that Sherlock was the youngest of three brothers, and that the eldest is Sherrinford. When Arthur Conan Doyle was trying to come up with the name of his great detective, one of the early names he considered was Sherrinford. Holmes mentions in "The Greek Interpreter" that his family were "country squires," and the eldest brother would have had to take over that position. Because Mycroft works in government and Sherlock is clearly not a country squire, Sherlockian scholars have speculated for decades that there must have been another brother. Mycroft says mysteriously in this episode, "You know what happened to the *other* one," referring to another Holmes brother.

NITPICKS There's no mention in the episode that Magnussen keeps his identity hidden, and yet when Sherlock is explaining to John how to break into Magnussen's private lift by deactivating the magnet on the swipe card, he said the security guards won't take Sherlock away because he might be Magnussen. If Magnussen takes that lift every day and the security guards are so close they'd be on him in an instant, don't they know what their boss looks like?

OOPS

- When Lady Elizabeth Smallwood's "file" shows up on screen, it says her first name is Alicia.
- Though it looks like Sherlock has dozens of pressure points, it's just the same six items scrolling past us quickly on the screen, as if, once again, the writers never realized their fans had a pause button on their remotes.

SOURCES

Aldridge, Gemma. *"Sherlock* Star Amanda Abbington Receives Death Threats After Her Character Mary Morstan Marries Watson." *The Mirror.* Online. January 12, 2014.

Anderson, Daniel. "Benedict Cumberbatch." *Uncut.* May 3, 2013.

BBC. *"Sherlock* Mini-Episode: Many Happy Returns — *Sherlock* Series 3 Prequel — BBC One." *YouTube* video, 7:12. December 24, 2013. https://www.youtube.com/watch?v=JwntNANJCOE.

"Being Benedict Cumberbatch — Interview with *The Standard.*"
The Standard. Online. February 22, 2014.

"Benedict Cumberbatch by Gary Oldman." *Interview Magazine*.
November 2013.

"Benedict Cumberbatch: My Mum Says I'm Like Sherlock." *Radio
Times*. Online. April 29, 2013.

Brown, Mike. "Benedict Cumberbatch on Alan Turing: 'He should
be on banknotes.'" *The Telegraph*. Online. November 1, 2014.

Chen, Anna. "Sherlock and Wily Orientals: Blind Banker, Episode 2
Review." *Madam Miaow Says*. Online. August 1, 2010.

Chivers, Tom. "Psychopaths: How Can You Spot One?" *The Telegraph*.
Online. April 6, 2014.

Cohen, Lisa J. "What Do We Know About Psychopathy?" *Psychology
Today*. Online. March 14, 2011.

Cumberbatch, Benedict. Filmmaker Chat. *Masterpiece*. Online.
November 1, 2010.

Davies, Caroline. "Queen's Birthday Honours List: Knights Outnumber
Dames Five to One." *The Guardian*. Online. June 12, 2015.

De Bertodano, Helena. "Martin Freeman: Fame, Family, and Fargo."
The Times Magazine. Online. April 13, 2014.

Dessau, Bruce. "Martin Freeman." *London Evening Standard*. October
2005. Reprinted as "Classic Interview: Martin Freeman" on *Beyond
the Joke*. Online.

Detz, Joanna. "Things You Probably Don't Want to Know about
Chocolate." *Progressive Charlestown*. Weblog. February 27, 2012.

Dodes, Rachel. "For *Hobbit* Star Martin Freeman, There Are No Small
Roles." *WSJ Speakeasy*. Online. December 14, 2012.

Dorris, Jesse. "Secrets, Leaks, and Sherlock." *Time*. October 28, 2013.

Doyle, Arthur Conan, Sir. *The Penguin Complete Sherlock Holmes*.
Foreword by Ruth Rendell. London: Penguin Books Ltd., 1930.
2009.

Elementary. TV Series. Executive Producers Robert Doherty, Craig
    Sweeny, Sarah Timberman, Carl Beverly, John Coles. CBS. 2012–.

Franklin, Oliver. "GQ&A: Martin Freeman on *The Hobbit, Sherlock*
    Erotica and Why He Hates Stylists." *GQ*. December 13, 2013.

Gatiss, Mark. "Sherlock: Mark Gatiss Interviews Martin Freeman."
    Radio Times. January 5, 2014.

Gilbert, Martin. "Coventry: What Really Happened." *Finest Hour* 141
    (Winter 2008–2009). Reprinted online at the Churchill Centre.

Gordon, Stuart. *The Encyclopedia of Myths and Legends*. London:
    Headline Book Publishing, 1993.

Griffin, Jennifer. "Martin Freeman Talks *Fargo*, the 'Everyman' Label &
    Our Taste for Darker TV." *Screen Spy*. Online. April 13, 2014.

Grimal, Pierre. *The Dictionary of Classical Mythology*. Oxford: Blackwell
    Publishers Ltd., 1996.

Hardy, Rebecca. "'People Care More about *X Factor* Than
    Homelessness': *The Office* star Martin Freeman on the Things That
    Tick Him Off." *Daily Mail*. Online. November 20, 2009.

"Hare Psychopathy Checklist." *Encyclopedia of Mental Disorders*. Online.

Hare, Robert D. "Psychopathy and Antisocial Personality Disorder:
    A Case of Diagnostic Confusion." *Psychiatric Times*. Online.
    February 1, 1996.

Harris, Tom. "How C-4 Works." *HowStuffWorks*. Online. June 20, 2002.

"In *Sherlock* a Classic Sleuth for the Modern Age." NPR.
    October 15, 2010.

"Interview with Benedict Cumberbatch and Martin Freeman."
    The Sunday Times. January 1, 2012.

Jefferies, Mark. "*Sherlock* Actor Benedict Cumberbatch Says He Almost
    Turned Down Iconic Role because He Worried It Might Be
    'Cheesy.'" *Mirror*. Online. February 14, 2014.

John, Emma. "On the Couch with Mr. Cumberbatch." *The Observer*.
    September 4, 2011.

Konnikova, Maria. "Stop Calling Sherlock a Sociopath! Thanks, a
    Psychologist." *iO9*. Online. August 11, 2012.

Kung, Michelle. "New Sherlock Holmes Benedict Cumberbatch on
    Portraying a Sociopath." *The Wall Street Journal*. October 22, 2010.

Leader, Michael. "Steven Moffat and Mark Gatiss Interview: *Sherlock*."
    Den of Geek! Online. July 21, 2010.

Lloyd Webber, Imogen. "It's to Be! Benedict Cumberbatch Will Play
    Hamlet in London." Broadway.com. Online. March 21, 2014.

Martin, Denise. "*Sherlock's* Amanda Abbington on the Finale, Mary's
    Big Secret, and Drunk Martin Freeman." *Vulture*. Online.
    February 3, 2014.

"Martin Freeman Talks Sherlock." *Empire Magazine*. Online.
    December 2011.

McCormack, Kirsty. "'Let's leave that a mystery': Martin Freeman
    May Have Already Married Amanda Abbington." *Sunday Express*.
    Online. April 12, 2014.

McIver, Peter J. "Churchill Let Coventry Burn to Protect His Secret
    Intelligence." *The Churchill Centre*. Online. Undated.

McLean, Craig. "Martin Freeman, Interview: 'Shakespeare invented
    Gollum.'" *The Telegraph*. July 28, 2014.

Mills, Nancy. "Benedict Cumberbatch Modernises Sherlock Holmes."
    USA Today. October 20, 2010.

Moffat, Steven. "Sherlock: Steven Moffat Interviews Benedict
    Cumberbatch." *Radio Times*. Online. January 1, 2014.

Moran, Caitlin. "My Love Affair with Sherlock." *The Times*.
    December 24, 2011.

O'Hare, Kate. "'Sherlock' Season 3: Amanda Abbington and Martin
    Freeman's Not-Wedding." *Zap2it*. Online. January 26, 2014.

Penny, Laurie. "No Shit, Sherlock." *New Statesman*. Online.
    August 3, 2010.

"Prison Tattoos and Their Secret Meanings." Likes.com.

The Private Life of Sherlock Holmes. DVD. Directed by Billy Wilder. 1970; MGM/UA Home Video, 2003.

Radish, Christina. "Amanda Abbington Talks *Sherlock*, Her Reaction to Finding Out Mary's Story, Working Alongside Her Real-Life Partner, Future Seasons, and More." *Collider*. Online. February 10, 2014.

Radish, Christina. "Benedict Cumberbatch Interview *Sherlock*; Also Talks About Steven Spielberg's *War Horse*." *Collider*. Online. October 3, 2010.

Rampton, James. "Sherlock's Amanda Abbington Admits Partner Martin Freeman Is One of Her Favourite Actors." *The Independent*. Online. December 30, 2013.

Reiher, Andrea. "Here's a Life-Sized Chocolate Benedict Cumberbatch — 'Chocobatch' — Just in Time for Easter!" *Zap2It*. Online. April 1, 2015.

Robinson, Jancis. "Bordeaux 2001 — the Forgotten Vintage?" JancisRobinson.com. Online. April 2, 2011.

Sandhu, Serina. "Baby Boy for Benedict Cumberbatch and Sophie Hunter." *The Independent*. Online. June 15, 2015.

Sawyer, Miranda. "Master of the Universe." *The Observer*. Online. April 17, 2005.

Sherlock, Series One. Created by Steven Moffat and Mark Gatiss. Burbank, CA: Warner Home Video, 2010. DVD.

Sherlock, Series Two. Created by Steven Moffat and Mark Gatiss. Burbank, CA: Warner Home Video, 2012. DVD.

Sherlock, Series Three. Created by Steven Moffat and Mark Gatiss. Burbank, CA: Warner Home Video, 2014. DVD.

"Sherlock: The Blind Banker." *I Will Not Love You Long Time*. Weblog. January 11, 2011.

Shoesmith, Ian, and Jon Kelly. "The Coventry Blitz 'Conspiracy.'" *BBC News*. Online. November 12, 2010.

Slocombe, Mike. "Façade and Dummy Houses at 23–24 Leinster Gardens, Paddington, London W2 above the Metropolitan and District Line." *London Landmarks*. Online. www.urban75.org. January 2007.

"Sophie Hunter and Benedict Cumberbatch Expecting Baby." *The Guardian*. Online. January 7, 2015.

Stevens, Christopher, "The REAL Warring Family Pair Who Inspired Mycroft and Sherlock: How Holmes's feud with His Scheming Sibling Is Based on the Troubled Past of the Creator's Own Brother." *MailOnline*. January 16, 2014.

Syme, Holger. "Steven Moffat, *Sherlock*, and Neo-Victorian Sexism." *dispositio*. Online. January 2, 2012.

Vincent, James. "How Sherlock-style Forensics Allowed Astrophysicists to Date This Monet Masterpiece." *The Independent*. Online. January 27, 2014.

Wightman, Catriona. "Martin Freeman: '*Sherlock* Is the Gayest Story Ever.'" *Digital Spy*. Online. May 23, 2011.

Wignall, Alice. "From *The Office* to *Nativity!*" *The Guardian*. Online. November 25, 2009.

Zobel, David. *The Science of TV's The Big Bang Theory*. Toronto: ECW Press, 2015.

ACKNOWLEDGMENTS

Many years ago, I was chatting with a fellow geek at a fan gathering, and she began talking excitedly about a man whose name I thought was some sort of joke. She insisted that Benedict Cumberbatch was his real name, and that some day he'd be a megastar and we'd all be talking about him. So thank you to Laurie Reid for first putting him on my radar.

A huge thank you to David Caron and Jack David at ECW Press for asking me to write this book, and to Crissy Calhoun for her editorial cheerleading, much-needed deadline extension, and all-round awesomeness during the process. Thanks also to my copy editor, Jen Knoch, and proofreader, Rachel Ironstone, for catching so many little things that would have otherwise been embarrassing. And thank you to Troy Cunningham for his beautiful design, Samantha Dobson for being such a fun publicist, and Aleksandra Lech for that gorgeous illustration on the cover.

While I was working on the book, I relied on some friends to help me clarify a few issues along the way. Thank you to Alison Marriott for helping me understand the visa situation in China for my commentary on "The Blind Banker"; to Darline Allen for explaining how a leftie could have shot a gun with his right hand in the same episode; to Dave Baker, who actually tried calling John Watson's phone number (which just rang busy, disappointing both of us); and to Simon Brown and Stacey Abbott for being my go-to British persons. Thanks to my friends and family who cheered me on and listened to me moan endlessly when my arms were aching from typing too much in a single day (especially Suzanne Kingshott, who got the brunt of it). To my beloved Slayage extended family, thank you for being so supportive of my writing — you have no idea how much your support means to me. And thank you also to the ladies of my Third Tuesday book club — Sue, Trish, Jeannette, Ashlie, and Darline — and the members of my Graphic Novel Group, who kept me reading other books as I was making my way through the Sherlock Holmes canon. And so much appreciation goes out to everyone who keeps me company on social media, making me laugh — and think — on a daily basis.

A huge thank you to Christopher Redmond, Peter Calamai, and Charles Prepolec for so affably weighing in with their thoughts on Sherlock. And I owe a huge debt of gratitude to the incredibly gracious Thelma Beam of The Bootmakers of

Toronto for putting me in touch with my three Sherlockian scholars.

This book was written throughout the summer and fall of 2014, with the music of Winged Victory for the Sullen's *Atomos XI* album playing almost constantly in the background. For the first time I wrote without my two feline muses, who'd been with me through the writing process of every one of my previous books. Instead I had two new furballs who did their best to replicate the requisite sitting on pages, chewing on my giant Penguin complete Sherlock Holmes edition, and making sure my notes were constantly flipped to the floor when I needed them. I want to thank my husband, Robert, for giving me writing time once again, and to my children, Sydney and Liam, who are finally old enough to start watching some of Mommy's shows with her. While my daughter loved watching *Sherlock*, my son still seems to prefer Time Lords to Great Detectives. Everyone's a critic.

Nikki Stafford, June 2015

nikki_stafford@yahoo.com

nikkistafford.blogspot.com

facebook.com/nikkistafford108

twitter.com/nikki_stafford

NIKKI STAFFORD is the author of the acclaimed Finding Lost series, as well as companion guides to *Buffy the Vampire Slayer*, *Alias*, *Angel*, and *Xena: Warrior Princess*. Nikki blogs regularly on her site, Nik at Nite (nikkistafford.blogspot.com). She lives in London, Ontario, where her mind palace is occupied by her husband and two children, several cats, and a few lizards, along with several million factoids that are probably useless and cause her to constantly forget why she just walked into a certain room. She should really declutter that brain attic.

ALSO BY NIKKI STAFFORD

Bite Me!: The Unofficial Guide to the World of Buffy the Vampire Slayer

Once Bitten: An Unofficial Guide to the World of Angel

Uncovering Alias: An Unofficial Guide

the *Finding Lost* series